THE NOBLE LEGACY

THE NOBLE LEGACY

Gilbert Clifford Noble, circa 1905

✦

The Story of Gilbert Clifford Noble, Cofounder of the Barnes & Noble and Noble & Noble Book Companies

As told by his granddaughter, Betty Noble Turner

iUniverse, Inc.

New York Lincoln Shanghai

THE NOBLE LEGACY
The Story of Gilbert Clifford Noble, Cofounder of the Barnes & Noble and Noble & Noble Book Companies

iUniverse books may be ordered through booksellers or by contacting:

iUniverse
2021 Pine Lake Road, Suite 100
Lincoln, NE 68512
www.iuniverse.com
1-800-Authors (1-800-288-4677)

ISBN-13: 978-0-595-37478-6 (pbk)
ISBN-13: 978-0-595-67508-1 (cloth)
ISBN-13: 978-0-595-81871-6 (ebk)
ISBN-10: 0-595-37478-6 (pbk)
ISBN-10: 0-595-67508-5 (cloth)
ISBN-10: 0-595-81871-4 (ebk)

Printed in the United States of America

For Jack Rice Turner, my wonderful husband and best friend, with love and appreciation for your constant encouragement and support.

For our children—Jay, Nancy, and Randall—and our eight precious grandchildren, Megan, Keni, Sam Rice, David, Joanie, Gracie, Jack, and Kate. This wonderful, talented, and lovable gang—our treasure.

And for my late parents, Orrel Baldwin and James Kendrick Noble, and my late brother, J. Kendrick Noble Jr., with love and gratitude for so much. The lives they led exemplified the Noble legacy.

Contents

Acknowledgments

Many, many people helped along the way, offering valuable information or support and encouragement, as I wrote this account of G. Clifford Noble's life. I will name just a few: my husband, Jack Rice Turner, who not only encouraged me to write this book, but also assisted in my research and traveled with me to places important in my grandfather's life; our sons, Randall and Jay, and Jay's wife, Nancy; my wonderful sister, Jean McAdams, who has kept me on task from the beginning and provided me with valuable information, and her husband, Bill; my late brother's daughter, Anne Noble; his son, Rick, and wife, Karen; and my former daughters-in-law, Clare Brown and Karen Turner. They have all been enthusiastic supporters of this effort.

Thanks, too, to my cousins Robert and Beth Baldwin; to Wendy Wakeman Stamer, who provided me with many family photographs; to Robert Cusick Noble, who started the whole thing when he compiled a family genealogy; and to William Adams Hunter IV, who published a wonderfully informative book, *The Family of William Adams.* I also owe special thanks to my late aunt, Vivien Noble Wakeman, who shared so many fascinating stories about her life with her father; to Reba Graham, who spent many hours copying and touching up photos and assisting in the design and layout of this book; and to Trent Moore for the time he spent on the computer—reordering photos and correcting errors on my computer. Finally, special thanks to Norma Jean Noble, my late brother's wife, who has been a tireless supporter and a valuable advisor throughout the writing of this book.

I also received invaluable editorial assistance and encouragement from Paula Silici, who assisted me in the beginning with much of the necessary editing and rewriting. Then there were those helpful people I met in Westfield, Massachusetts at the public library who provided me with excellent information, and those I have come to know more recently, such as my new friend Carol Noble Benner, the force behind the Noble-Warriner Web site.

It was my special friend the Rev. Ken Smith, a former fellow national AARP board member from Chicago, who put me in contact with Nancy Follett Waichler. With Nancy's help I was able to locate Steve Waichler, her son, and Bob Follett, her brother, both of whom provided me with some invaluable and otherwise unavailable information about the Follett Company and its relationship to Barnes & Noble.

Thanks also to many friends who kept me focused on completing the book and remained interested in its progress: Donald and Susan Taft, Mark and Kathy Klein, Norman and Susan Ransleben, Charles and Linda Zahn, Peggy Willmott, John D. Roberts, Greg and Kathy Sales, Lisa Brunsvold, Mary Jo Currey, Taddy and Edith McAllister, Sunny Castor, Patty Mueller, Gemma Just, Sandra Thomas, Susan Yerkes, Tony Shioleno, Gary Looper, Don Stewart, Bea Hanson, Chuck Leven, Ruth Ann Montgomery, and Lou Warren. Finally, thanks to my many childhood friends from Yonkers, including Vail Taylor, Carol Butts Kilbourne, and Ralph Mills; and my other good friends, too numerous to name individually, in Corpus Christi and Port Aransas.

I should also mention those family members who are no longer with us but who provided much of the substance of this book and the reasons for writing it. My late parents and brother certainly head this group.

Thanks to each of you who have inspired and helped me complete this memoir.

May you all find this book a happy and historical read about an extraordinary individual whose story *did* need telling.

Introduction

The joy of the Lord is your strength.

—Nehemiah 8:10

◆   ◆   ◆

On June 6, 1936, Gilbert Clifford Noble died unexpectedly at his home in Yonkers, New York. He was seventy-two years old. In "An Obituary Note," *The Publishers Weekly* referred to him as "one of the deans of publishers."[1] Notables in the publishing industry joined family and friends at Clifford's funeral, and family members received letters and calls from hundreds of friends, business associates, and acquaintances throughout the country. Clifford's death dealt a stinging and lasting sense of loss to the many hundreds who had known and loved him, and its impact was strongly felt in the book-publishing industry and in his family for years to come.

The Noble Legacy is Gilbert Clifford Noble's story. It is the true, heretofore untold account of the visionary cofounder and namesake of the original Barnes & Noble and Noble & Noble book companies. Clifford Noble was the leading force behind the creation and early development of both book houses. He was a gifted individual who, even in childhood, could take ideas from anywhere and turn them into moneymaking ventures. He was the consummate risk taker, a man willing to make difficult decisions when he believed he had the right information or when he was convinced an opportunity warranted the risk. He also had the tenacity and self-confidence needed to persevere in difficult and challenging circumstances.

But Clifford's successes were rooted in much more than his entrepreneurial spirit. His real strength lay in his strong faith and character. He believed, as the Bible had taught him, that "with God, all things are possible." The reader may find that this account of Clifford Noble's life focuses almost exclusively on his favorable qualities. If the absence of serious human frailties is thought to be a negative, then so be it. But listen to this story, and then decide for yourself.

Clifford was the patriarch of a close-knit family. His life revolved around his wife and children. His faith and his family were his top priorities. He shared his beliefs and values, as well as the rituals and traditions of life, with his children, preparing them to become successful and secure in their own right. It is often said that there are only two lasting bequests we can give our children: one is roots; the other, wings. Clifford Noble gave his sons and daughters both.

Clifford was my paternal grandfather. I adored him when I was a young child, although I would not fully appreciate his legacy until I was grown. But I vividly remember him as an amiable, regal-looking older gentleman, medium in height and distinctive for his snow-white hair, neatly clipped moustache, sparkling blue eyes, and impeccable but simple manner of dress. He walked with a fashionable, dark wooden cane, and I often wondered whether he really needed one—although it certainly added to his imposing demeanor!

I was just a few years old when my grandfather died, but I loved him because I knew that I had been very important to him. Clifford had a memorable way of making people feel important and good about themselves, regardless of who they were, and he took great delight in empowering people to accomplish amazing feats. No wonder he was so well loved and successful. He was, after all, a gentle-man—a strikingly honorable man who was kind, caring, and fun-loving—and I cherish the warm feelings and vivid memories that I have of him. My "Pa Pa" was a special person indeed.

Clifford Noble, the son of hardworking, lower-middle-class farmers, grew up in the small New England farming community of Westfield, Massachusetts, in the aftermath of the Civil War. His parents—abolitionists and social activists—inspired his lifetime respect for the sanctity of diversity and his commitment to the significant social causes of the day. Although Clifford's parents attempted to persuade him to choose life on the farm, Clifford attended Harvard College, graduated with honors, and moved to New York City, where he carved out an illustrious career in the book industry.

This book contains many personal anecdotes about Clifford and his ventures. The beliefs and values he held dear, and the historical context in which he lived, were the backdrop for the establishment and continued growth of his two premier book houses—companies that not only outlived him, but probably outgrew his own ambitions.

Although neither of Clifford's companies is owned by any members of the Noble family today, unless of course they own its publicly traded stock, the current chairman of Barnes & Noble, Leonard Riggio, came from much the same modest beginnings as Pa Pa. And many of the decisions and customer-friendly innovations that Riggio has made in his multibillion-dollar organization reflect the beliefs and values instituted by my grandfather in the original Barnes & Noble and Noble & Noble book companies.

Precious little is known about the origins of these two companies or about Clifford Noble himself, although countless books about other successful individuals fill the shelves of our libraries and bookstores today. So I wondered whether readers might find another such book of any interest. But the more I researched Clifford's life and achievements, and the more I talked with people who knew him or knew about him, the more I believed that his story needed to be told.

The available literature on other notable booksellers suggests that Clifford lived his life and built his businesses in a manner that serves as a living testament to why his name and legacy have endured. Many business schools today are beginning to teach their students that the business world is moving back toward employing and promoting people of verifiable character—men and women with exceptional business skills and strong personal values. The business school at Harvard, for example, is requiring all students to take a course on ethics and leadership. This revival is designed to prepare students to deal more effectively with the morally complex business issues they will likely face. It also emphasizes those qualities that contributed to Clifford's success. While his story may serve as a historical account of his time, and of the two great book companies he founded, it may also serve as a useful manual for today's budding entrepreneurs.

If Pa Pa were here today to tell you about his life and legacy, he would probably begin with his typical, modest self-introduction: "I was a poor country boy from a small New England town who was just plain lucky." His life story, however, is full of examples to the contrary. Luck was only a minor factor in Clifford's lifetime of achievement.

In 1936, looking ahead to the fiftieth anniversary of his graduation from Harvard, G. Clifford Noble reminisced about his life and achievements. In a handwritten report that he sent to his class secretary just a few short weeks before the celebration, he reflected on his life's work and experiences and reconfirmed what mattered most to him. Sadly, Clifford died the very day he was to leave for Cambridge to attend that class reunion, but his thoughts are all the more worth repeating.

Fifty years ago, the syllables are jeweled with the laughter and tears of life...each year a bead...not turned and polished monotonously so that one exactly matches another...but rather have they been for me like those little wooden balls my children strung together in nursery days, some rough, some smooth, to hang around their mother's neck. The most wonderful thing about it is that this string that bound them all (and us) together never broke.

Today my happiness is kindred to the memory of that tie, for I can look back and see that the work and care which has run through each bead has never broken. I am, at the fiftieth year, as I began, a book publisher of educational books—with my steadfast faith, my wife (who graduated the same year from Vassar College), my home and my family, all my children, and all my grandchildren close beside me, and the dreams of that first year come true.[2]

As one of the grandchildren of G. Clifford Noble, let me tell you about him.

Betty Noble Turner

1

The Budding Entrepreneur

Clifford Noble, age 12

*If you want to succeed, you should strike out
on new paths rather than travel worn paths of accepted success.*

—John D. Rockefeller Sr.

◆   ◆   ◆

The seeds of greatness are sometimes planted at an early age. In Clifford Noble's case, those nascent little seeds took the form of chicken feed.

It was a beautiful, brisk autumn morning in Westfield, Massachusetts. Twelve-year-old Clifford Noble was flying his homemade kite near his home with his nine-year-old brother Howard, when they heard the shouting of a neighboring farmer who was approaching them from across a nearby field.

"Have you two boys seen my chickens?" the farmer shouted. Clifford thought he seemed upset. The farmer repeated his question, and the boys shook their heads as he came closer.

But Clifford was curious. Keeping his eyes on the soaring kite as it dipped and glided through the beautiful azure sky past cotton-like clouds, he replied, "Your chickens? No, sir. Why?"

"Because they're on the loose again, and no doubt causing havoc in the neighborhood." Looking quite perturbed, the farmer scratched his head and thought a moment. Clifford's interest was piqued, but he said nothing, and Howard, worried that the farmer was very angry, tried to remain inconspicuous.

The man looked out across the field. "Say, you boys wouldn't want to do a job for me, would you? I know you're busy flying that kite, but if you can round up my chickens, I'll let you have every last one of them. Get 'em out of my hair for good this time. What do you say?"

Jobs of any kind were scarce in post–Civil War Westfield, Massachusetts, especially for children. No doubt that reality fueled young Clifford's amazing aptitude for identifying entrepreneurial opportunities in the most unlikely of places.

Clifford knew the chickens couldn't have strayed far, and he sensed a great business opportunity. "Yes, sir!" he cried excitedly, quickly reeling in his ball of kite string. "Of course we'll do it. Why, my brother and I can round those chickens up in no time." The farmer nodded his approval, and Clifford turned to his brother. "Come on, Howard," he said, waving his hand and beckoning to Howard to follow. "We've got a job to do."

Watching the boys busy themselves with their task, the farmer shoved his hands in his pockets, shook his head, and smiled. *Now there's a likely pair of youngsters,* he said to himself. *That older boy seems to have a good head on his shoulders. We'll see what he can do…*

None of the four Noble children received an allowance, but Clifford, the second oldest, had learned early how to transform even the simplest of situations into lucrative economic ventures. It had taken him only a few moments to size up the financial potential of the farmer's proposal, one he happily realized also provided him with a good chance to do something helpful for a neighbor.

With Clifford in the lead, the boys ran to the chicken coops in their backyard and stuffed their faded blue overall pockets with chicken feed. Then they set out to find the recalcitrant hens. *They must be around here somewhere,* Clifford thought, and said to Howard, "Let's go over to the east side of that vacant field and look for them." And within a few short minutes, Clifford, pointing at the disordered flock pecking randomly at the barren ground, shouted, "Look, Howard. Just as I thought. There they are."

With their pockets bulging, the boys ran across the stubble and cautiously approached the chickens. Clifford quickly showed his little brother how to scatter a thin trail of feed from the vacant property back to their family's coops.

It wasn't long before the hungry hens discovered the grain and began to peck their way to the Nobles' yard. In an hour or so, the boys had managed to secure all of the wayward birds in their new home. Clifford and Howard jubilantly claimed ownership of the hens. Watching from a distance, the incredulous farmer smiled broadly, genuinely impressed by the boys' resourceful activity. *Can't hurt to give the lads a chance,* he thought, walking back to his barn. *And it looks as though my hunch paid off.*

"We did it!" Clifford cried, laughing and slapping Howard on his back as they locked up the last of the chickens. "Well-done, little brother," he said proudly. "You and I did a great job getting those chickens rounded up so quickly. Don't you think we make a good team?"

But Howard didn't look too pleased. It was sometimes hard to figure out what Clifford had in mind, and more than once Howard had come out on the short end of the stick. Dubiously eyeing the birds, he asked, "What are we going to do with them now that we've got them? They're all dirty and smelly, and somebody's going to have to clean up after them and feed them. I certainly don't want that job, Clifford. Besides, what do you think mother and father are going to say when they find out?"

Clifford was a little annoyed that Howard, the more conservative of the two, couldn't see the big picture, as was often the case. "Oh, you worry too much," he chided. "Those dirty, smelly hens are going to make us both rich. Just you wait and see. We're going to make our parents very proud of us."

In the days that followed, Clifford and a still dubious Howard spent many hours after school cleaning the henhouse and rearranging roosts. They were even successful in securing their father's assistance in building a few more laying cubbyholes to accommodate their rather large new flock. They used scrap lumber that they'd salvaged from yet another neighbor's yard. Once their work was finished and their hens were accustomed to their new home and happily laying eggs, Clifford let Howard in on the details of their new business venture.

"We're going to start an egg production, sales, and delivery business," he told Howard in a very resolute tone. "What do you think?"

After contemplating the idea for a moment or two, Howard found it less than appealing. He felt that he had always been more practical than his brother, so he asked the obvious question, "But who's going to *buy* our eggs?"

Clifford explained his plan with just a hint of impatience in his voice. "Everybody, Howard. All the people who live in our neighborhood. Just think. This will be the first business of its kind in our neighborhood. We'll be filling a void, so we should be able to attract a lot of customers. We're going to take orders, sell our eggs directly to our buyers for a penny apiece, and then we'll charge them an extra ten cents for making home delivery. We won't have the expense of paying someone else to make deliveries for us. We'll do that. But that's a reasonable price, don't you think, and it certainly means more profit for us. Besides, can you think of anyone else in our neighborhood who is offering this kind of convenience?"

Of course Howard couldn't think of anyone either. He mulled over his brother's rationale, not yet fully comprehending all that was involved.

Both boys had helped out for years around the family farm doing a variety of chores. They had fed their parents' chickens, collected and sized the eggs, cleaned the henhouse, and even reluctantly wrung a chicken neck or two when that was called for. But neither boy had actually managed his *own* business, no less begun one. Still, Clifford found *that* idea to be immensely appealing.

"Think about it," he continued. "We'll have our *own* company—the C&H Egg Company! C for Clifford and H for Howard. Get it?" Once Howard discovered that his name—or first initial at least—would be part of the company name, he decided that perhaps his brother's newest idea did have merit after all. He grinned. "Of course I get it," he chided Clifford. "Sounds like a promising idea and an easy way to make money. I'm ready to get started." An amused Clifford chuckled to himself about Howard's sudden revelation and gloated over his idea. Clifford was already learning about the value and power of a company's name.

As it happened, a neighbor had recently discarded a primitive-looking wooden wagon, which the boys salvaged and promptly put to work. They made the necessary repairs and painted "C&H" on the side of the wagon in large red letters. Their parents, delighted with their sons' ingenuity and newest venture, provided them with a list of likely egg buyers who lived within walking distance of their home. The boys used that list as they walked throughout the area taking orders.

They received an enthusiastic reception wherever they went and were able to start their business earlier than they had anticipated.

Clifford and Howard made their home deliveries by pulling their loaded wagon through the neighborhood right behind the kindhearted and talkative old milkman, Addison Noble, as he made his daily deliveries in the neighborhood. Addison was apparently no relation to the boys, but they all got along quite well together. Addison Noble drove a one-horse, two-wheeled, low-hung metal milk cart filled with ten-quart canisters from which he would ladle milk into the covered basins, pans, and pitchers that his customers left on their porches.[1] The boys would follow right behind, leaving their fresh, bagged eggs alongside the milk whenever they and Addison shared a customer.

Addison never ceased to be impressed by the boys' hard work and ingenuity. One day he laughingly told them, "You are amazing young fellows. And I'm beginning to think that I'd better look out—or you'll be taking over *my* business!" The boys were quick to tell him that their egg business was all *they* could hope to manage.

"Besides," Clifford reassured him, "we like working *with* you."

In no time at all, the C&H Egg Company was the talk of the community. Neighbors recognized an extremely credible operation when they saw one, and the boys basked in their newfound success. The best thing of all was the tidy financial sum their business venture was generating. Some neighbors urged them to expand operations to gain extra business and additional income, a suggestion which excited Howard and Clifford and one that they soon decided to consider.

After discussing their proposed expansion and ways in which they could make it work, they agreed on a marketing strategy that would reward regular customers who referred new customers to them. To announce their promotion, the boys designed, produced and then posted their colorful, hand-lettered flyers on their family's fence.

The boys made the flyers from paper scraps that they rescued from the trash at the local newspaper office. Later in life, Clifford would joke that his career in publishing began in a trash bin, motivated by his desire to save a few cents. But he always acknowledged that the experience had proved to be a good lesson in the value of frugality and creative product promotion.

The boys delivered similar handbills to their home-delivery customers, then topped off their promotion with a simple advertising jingle that they wrote, and recited to neighbors along the way.

Bring us a new customer and your reward will be
A half-dozen eggs delivered for free.
It's a pretty good bargain; you'll be helping us, too.
And all our new customers will be grateful to you!

Clifford was convinced that their original promotional ditty was a winner, and even Howard loved it. Some of their neighbors were not so impressed, but the boys' lively, good-natured performance guaranteed the success of their marketing effort. In fact, the young egg merchants were overwhelmed by the enthusiastic response. Neighbors actually sought them out to add the names of friends to the brothers' growing customer list. Almost immediately they built up such a large customer base that they had to stop taking any new orders.

For the remainder of the year, the two brothers were owners-managers of an extremely lucrative egg production and sales operation. They were not only able to pay all their operating expenses from their earnings, but they also generated several dollars of profit each month—an impressive bundle of money which they divided equally. *This business has been a good thing for both of us,* thought Clifford, immensely proud of their success and more than a little pleased with *his* own business acumen.

Realizing early on that he needed to begin saving his earnings, Clifford opened his first savings account in a local Westfield bank and successfully persuaded Howard to do likewise.

The C&H Egg Company gave Clifford his first real taste of what was involved with building a successful new business. He learned that he had to identify his market and his competition, price his product accordingly, design an effective sales and marketing strategy, determine his likely costs and profit, and then decide whether or not the projected earnings would be worth the cost and time the undertaking would require. In Clifford's case, it certainly was.

But success often has its downside. As their business prospered, the boys finally acknowledged that they had a serious problem. "School," Clifford solemnly informed Howard one day, "is interfering with our business. It takes so much of our time that we don't have enough free hours to bag our eggs and make all of our deliveries."

Clifford's glum analysis discouraged Howard. He was used to following his older brother's lead. "So what do we do now?" he asked soulfully. "You're the one who usually has the good ideas."

"Maybe we should hire someone to help us," Clifford suggested. "Or maybe *we* should just leave school early every day so we *do* have time to make our deliveries."

Howard brightened at the latter suggestion. "I like *that* idea," he said. "Clifford, I *really* like that idea."

But the boys' attentive mother, just happening to overhear the discussion, quickly intervened. "You have it backwards, my dear boys," she told them sternly. She'd been watching the growing egg business take more and more of her sons' time away from studies and family chores. "It's your *business* that's interfering with your schoolwork, not the other way around," she said. "From now on, I'll be running the egg business, and you two will be spending your time doing schoolwork."

Although disappointed with their mother's decision, the boys took it in stride, realizing it would do them no good to argue. Not only had their popular neighborhood egg business elevated their status in the community, it had also built them a fine reputation among their neighbors as creative, hardworking young men. In addition, the enterprise had given them, especially Clifford, an enormous amount of self-confidence. Clifford had learned with absolute certainty that moneymaking opportunities could often be found in the most unexpected places. It was just a matter of recognizing them and then devising ways to make them profitable.

Mrs. Moseley's Pies

As popular and highly respected as the Noble boys had become, the brothers were also known to be fun-loving, mischievous pranksters. "Typical boys" was how most of the neighbors described them, although there were a few who often voiced less flattering observations, despite the boys' frequent helpful deeds.

Some of Westfield's best cooks lived in a section of town that the boys had to pass through as they made their way home from school each day. Knowing which days were baking days, and always alert to the tantalizing aroma of freshly baked pies cooling on back windowsills, it rarely took the boys long to find a pie. It took them an even shorter time to pilfer one and devour it.

One afternoon on their way home from school, the boys passed Mrs. Moseley's house. They smelled the irresistible aroma of juicy McIntosh apples cooling in a flaky, sugary piecrust, a pastry specialty of Mrs. Moseley. McIntosh apples were Clifford's favorite. They grew abundantly in the area, and he loved their tart, fresh taste. Even as an adult he would continue to be partial to that kind of apple, and he later planted a small orchard of McIntosh apples in the backyard of his home in Yonkers, New York, so that the fruit was always readily available.

As the pie's aroma reached the boys' sensitive nostrils, they stopped abruptly and looked knowingly at each other. "Let's go," they whispered in unison, hurrying off to the rear of Mrs. Moseley's yard.

"Got it!" Howard exclaimed a few suspenseful moments later as he snatched one of the still-warm pies from the windowsill. With Howard carefully balancing the prize, the boys quickly made their way to safe territory to devour their plunder. The fact that they were covered with pastry and the remains of the pie when they finished merely made them laugh sheepishly at one another. Then they raced home to get cleaned up.

(Clifford's conscience must have played havoc with his enjoyment of the moment, but not enough, it seems, to stem his craving for one of Mrs. Moseley's pies.)

Mrs. Moseley would quickly realize that she was not the only victim of pie theft. Some of the other ladies in the neighborhood began to talk among themselves, comparing notes about their missing pies and speculating about who some of the culprits might be. Of course, they had a pretty solid notion, especially when it came to the Noble boys, but because the boys were so well liked, the women never reported the thefts to their parents. They simply kept on baking pies, although they now let them cool in safer, more secure locations, only occasionally leaving one out to tempt their favorite young rascals.

The Pond

Throughout his life, Clifford Noble was addicted to the outdoors, especially when the long, frigid winters stole through New England. It was then that he and Howard, the two lifetime soul mates, would make their way to the large, spring-fed duck pond located about five hundred feet west of their home. The frozen pond made an excellent site for ice-skating, and naturally became the popular neighborhood skating rink.

In the winter, the boys spent their time at the pond trying to skate, or at least trying to remain upright on their crude, wooden skates. Because the skate blades were fastened awkwardly to the boys' boots with long screws and straps, the skates never fitted very well and frequently fell off. It seems more than likely that Clifford Noble developed his extraordinary, lifelong patience at that frozen pond, fastening and refastening those ornery skates just to have the short-lived, exhilarating experience of gliding over the ice like a ship in full sail.

In the early summer, when the fields were laden with lush foliage, the pond became the watering hole for numerous varieties of wildlife, including geese, raccoons, squirrels, and even deer. Clifford, Howard, and many of their classmates would gather at their "zoo," as they had fondly dubbed the area.[2] They made it their favorite, regular meeting place.

It was at the zoo that Clifford would often spend a half hour or so mimicking the geese. He'd flap his arms, hiss loudly, and then defiantly charge them to the delight of the other children, who watched from afar. But the geese rarely moved, preferring to stand their ground and mock his attempts to invade their territory.[3] Clifford's bravery however, such as it was, earned him due notice and endeared him to the neighborhood youngsters.

Winter Jobs

Westfield winters could be exceedingly harsh. Heavy snowstorms frequently blanketed the ground with several feet of snow. The Noble boys relished the opportunities that the freezing weather offered and often skated to school atop the snow crust. They were able to zip across the fields and over the fences that were covered by snow drifts and reach school in record time.

After each snow storm, the public-minded Tom Moseley, a local dairy farmer and chairman of the three-member Selectmen board, worked to keep the sidewalks passable. He maneuvered his v-shaped, horse-drawn snowplow down Union Street and across the snowbound pedestrian pathways.[4] Since most people had limited transportation and walked everywhere, this courtesy endeared Moseley to the neighborhood.

At times the Noble boys, sensing another job opportunity, offered to assist Moseley after school, by moving whatever obstacles got in his way and by sweeping clean the freshly plowed areas. A grateful Mr. Moseley usually rewarded them with a few pennies for their help.

Eventually springtime came, and none too soon for the winter-weary Westfield residents. Bright yellow daffodils and lavender crocuses emerged from the once-frozen ground to herald the arrival of the warmer weather. The ubiquitous red robins—harbingers of spring, busily made their rounds through the open fields searching for food. As the snow melted and shoveling opportunities ended, the boys continued to assist their neighbors. On weekends they stayed busy with yard mowing, raking, weeding, and watering; jobs that provided them with some extra pocket change and some very appreciative neighbors.

The Swimming Hole

One of Clifford's favorite summertime haunts was the swimming hole; a natural stream located on the Sandy Mill Brook, just a short distance from the Nobles' home. Clifford, his friends, and his two brothers all loved to go skinny-dipping there. Clifford was usually the first one in. He would cannonball into the cold water amid the loud and enthusiastic cries of his group. Then he would happily paddle around, shouting at the others to join him. They were usually quick to follow, and they'd spend the remainder of the day together, playing water games and tag.

One day, Howard left for home early and accidentally gathered up Clifford's pants with his own towels. Clifford, hoping that Howard would realize his gaffe, anxiously waited for his brother to return to the stream, but to no avail. So the disheartened, tearful, and buck naked Clifford was left with but one painful choice. He had to stealthily make his way home along deserted paths, terrified that his sister, Julia, and her friends would see him—a prospect he knew he'd be ridiculed about for years to come.

To cover his nudity, Clifford broke off limbs from some of the trees along the way and tried using their leaves to cover himself, but without much success. It was embarrassing for Clifford, a modest teenager, to have to subject himself to the uncertainty of meeting people in that state of undress. But he finally reached home without incident.

Despite the happy outcome, Clifford never let Howard forget the humiliating mishap. He perpetrated countless payback pranks on his apologetic younger brother for many years thereafter. "Accidents happen, Clifford," Howard would invariably remind him, while extolling the virtue of forgiveness, but Clifford seemed to relish having a few chances to good-naturedly rib his little brother.

Fishing at the Swimming Hole

A dam controlled the flow of water into the swimming hole so that there was usually sufficient water for swimming and fishing. The nearby grist mills and saw mills, however, also depended on the water for power. When the mills needed more water, workers closed a set of wooden gates that diverted the water through a canal to the mills. As soon as the mills stopped operating for the day, the gates were raised and the flow of water to the swimming hole resumed.

On its way to the swimming hole, the water cascaded onto a fifty-square-foot wooden apron over which a wooden bridge for road traffic passed. In spawning season, large numbers of fish would jump the dam and begin swimming upstream.[5] One day this migration caught the imagination of the Noble boys and inspired yet another enterprising activity.

Early one morning when no one else was around and traffic on the bridge was nonexistent, Clifford and Howard closed the gates, leaving only a small amount of water on the apron. To their delight, they discovered that the sun-drenched shallows were teeming with hundreds of thrashing fish, glittering like a sea of jewels. It was quite a sight.

"Wow!" Howard cried. "Just look at that. I've never seen so many fish."

Gazing down at all those lovely fish flopping about for the taking, Clifford recognized a new opportunity.

"Do you realize that if we can catch them, we can sell them and make a lot of money?" Clifford said. "We just need something to put them in." The boys looked around, but nothing came to mind. Then Clifford had an idea. "Take off your pants, Howard," he said firmly, "and tie the legs together like I'm doing. We'll use our pants like bags." Howard was embarrassed by the idea, but since there was no one else around and he had not thought of a better way to catch the fish, he agreed and followed his brother's lead.

Hopping on one foot and then on the other, the boys quickly removed their trousers. They tied their pant legs together, then scooped up and bagged the frantic fish. They probably "caught" about three bushels.

The boys laid out their catch on a low, cool grassy spot by the stream. Then they scrambled back into their pants and—Clifford's idea—ran home to secure some pails and buckets to carry the fish home in.

The boys' take was so abundant that, even after giving some of the fish to their mother to fix for supper that evening, they still had plenty left over. They sold the extra fish to their neighbors and pocketed a profit of about $15.00.

"Do you realize," Clifford said, as he and Howard counted their money that night just before bedtime, "that we probably made more money in a few short hours today than our father nets in a whole week?"

Lessons Learned

Needless to say, from then on "fishing" was the boys' favorite avocation, until their parents, questioning the legality of the boys' technique, put an end to the enterprise. But the boys came away from the venture having learned some valuable lessons about making money.

Clifford in particular learned a great deal about the importance of recognizing opportunities and having a doable action plan for transforming them into a steady stream of profits. And he was getting quite proficient at doing just that.

Learning to create his own money-making opportunities out of what appeared to others to be seemingly ordinary situations was exciting to Clifford; his egg business and his fish-catching operation had convinced him that the future belonged to entrepreneurs. And G. Clifford Noble was certain he was one.

2

Roots

*We should rejoice in the accomplishments of those before us, be proud of the heritage
that we inherit, but be always vigilant that the future is ours alone to make.*

—Eleanor Roosevelt
—David B. Roosevelt, *Grandmere*

◆   ◆   ◆

Clifford's veracious character and proclivity for risk taking and entrepreneurial
activity could have been predicted from an early age, given his remarkable
family history.

According to Lucius Boltwood's *History and Genealogy of the Family of Thomas
Noble*, G. Clifford Noble, an eighth-generation Noble in America, was a descendant of Thomas Noble, "an emigrant ancestor and progenitor of the largest family in the United States bearing the name Noble."[1] The exact birthplace of
Thomas Noble, son of Thomas and Rachel Gardner Noble, is unknown, but the
general concurrence is that he was born in England, probably as early as 1632.
We do know for certain, however, that he died in Westfield, Massachusetts, on
January 20, 1704.[2]

When Thomas Noble was only about twenty-one years old, he left home and
joined a group of Puritans to sail from London to Boston Harbor on one of several large sailing sloops. The Puritans' mission was to help those who had already
made the hazardous voyage across the Atlantic Ocean and established the Massachusetts Bay Colony. During Thomas's ten-week voyage through 5,000 miles of
unmerciful seas, many of his shipmates died, but the determined, self-reliant
young man survived.

The experience helped Thomas acquire many of the skills and values—and the mindset—he would need to overcome the difficulties and challenges he'd likely face in the new world. Shaken and physically weakened by the ordeal, he was nevertheless optimistic about his future. Upon his arrival in port, he quickly disembarked the battered vessel, eager to plant his feet firmly on American soil.

Drake's out-of-print *History of Boston, (p. 331)* confirms that Thomas Noble became an official inhabitant of Boston on January 5, 1653, and that almost immediately, he migrated to Springfield, Massachusetts, and became one of Springfield's earliest settlers.[3] On November 1, 1660, he married seventeen-year-old Hannah Warriner, the only daughter of William and Joanna (Scant) Warriner.[4]

In addition to working in agriculture, Thomas is thought to have been a tailor and a member of the Merchant Tailors' Company. He earned quite a good reputation as a tailor and worked part time at the local fur trading post. The post was run by John Pynchon, one of the original founders of Springfield.

Although Thomas had brought ample farm and household supplies with him from England, he wasted little time running up an account for food, sewing supplies, and dry goods at the trading post. He was known to be a free spender who lived beyond his means and he gradually became heavily indebted to Mr. Pynchon.[5] He even borrowed money from Pynchon to make a trip back to England that he was unable to repay.

Finally, in 1667, the General Court of the area ruled that Thomas had taken undue advantage of Pynchon and that Pynchon deserved restitution. The court ruled that Noble turn over his home in Springfield, and all his lands to Pynchon.[6] That must have been a difficult and embarrassing time for Thomas, and one that would have discouraged the heartiest of the early settlers. But he prided himself on being a survivor and became more determined than ever to improve his circumstances and provide for his growing family.

Thomas joined a committed group of early pioneer settlers and their families who were headed for the undeveloped, fertile Connecticut Valley, which was nestled at the foot of the Berkshires in Massachusetts, to begin a new settlement. The area was known to the Indians as *Woronoco,* meaning "it is fat hunting," because of its plentiful game.[7] The area was one of the best localities for beaver known to the Indians and the settlers. More skins came from Woronoco than any other location so the Indians used the area as a market place for their furs.[8]

The area was later renamed Westfield because it was the most westerly settlement in Massachusetts.[9]

The first of several deeds of land in Woronoco, all of which had been purchased by its earliest settlers from the Indians, was legalized in October 1660.

Town records show that the town granted ten acres of land for his farmhouse, an additional ten acres of lowland, and another seven acres that were customarily distributed to the original settlers according to the size of their families.

On his thirty acres of pristine Connecticut Valley frontier property, Thomas enjoyed a plentiful and diverse supply of wild game that included deer, bear, moose, otter, and beaver. Fish of all kinds were also plentiful in the nearby streams, and various kinds of game birds abounded in the area.

With help from his friends, Thomas built his new farmhouse and raised corn, beans, and pumpkins. He also hunted and fished and tended the few farm animals that the Selectmen of the community had given him.

His home was located on a picturesque hillside, just west of the Lane traprock quarries. It was built on what is now known as East Mountain Road between Westfield and Springfield on land that would later become home to the Westfield State Sanatorium. That property is now the home of the state-owned Western Massachusetts Hospital.[10]

Life was not always tranquil in this earthly paradise. Thomas and his young family soon discovered the perils of living in an area isolated from the center of town and exposed to the harshness of raw nature and the elements.

Thomas's homestead was vulnerable to Indian attacks during the period of King Philip's War when raids and skirmishes raged through many New England towns and villages, and the friendly trade relations that the settlers had initially enjoyed with the local Indians gradually deteriorated. Tensions between the two groups intensified as the Indians found that the white settlers were encroaching on their land and they became determined to drive them out. Indian attacks on the settlers became more frequent and more brutal, forcing many families to give up their homes and move closer to town.

Thomas stubbornly refused to relocate, choosing instead to protect his homestead. From his personal history, comes the story of a harrowing experience he once had with the hostile Waranoke Indian chief named Gray Lock.[11] It's a story that is reported by Boltwood, but one that generations of Nobles no doubt embellished some, and one that they dearly loved to retrieve from the seemingly bottomless depths of the family archives to recount to their children and grandchildren. The rapt and wide-eyed youngsters were equally happy to gather at their feet to hear it. The tale was one of Clifford's favorites. He often relayed it to his own fascinated children, who begged him for many retellings.

The Tale of Gray Lock

One dark, starless, cold winter evening, so the story goes, Thomas Noble finished a sumptuous meal of roasted venison and homegrown vegetables, praised his wife's culinary skills, and took a last sip of his after-supper herbal tea. After draining his cup, he looked proudly at his young family and smiled. *Life is good*, he told himself, thankful he had decided to settle in the area.

He watched with loving affection as his wife Hannah carried the last of the supper dishes to the wash bucket near the corner of their primitive kitchen. How fortunate he was, he mused, that the Lord had blessed him with a loving family that was now tucked safely indoors, warm, free from illness, and well fed.

Yes, it was true that there had been frequent reports of Indian raids nearby, and Thomas knew well enough that complacency in this untrammeled wilderness could get one killed. But thankfully, serious trouble had stayed away from his door and he was confident that his family would continue to be safe.

Pushing back from the table, the rather tall, distinguished-looking Thomas methodically strolled through his modest frame home, checking the wooden shutters and carefully adjusting each one to ensure a snug fit against the blustering, cold wind.

"Hannah," he called, "when you're finished putting everything away, kindly gather the children for evening prayers."

When all the domestic chores had been completed, Hannah rounded up the children. Thomas threw several stout lengths of wood on the roaring fire. Then he bade everyone kneel before the hearth's comforting warmth on the soft cushions that his wife had made from scrap material and animal fur.

Thomas began to recite the evening's devotions in his deep resonant voice. "Our dear Heavenly Father..." But before he could say another word, the front door swung open with such force that it shook the entire dwelling, sending the startled Thomas straight to his feet.

Terrified screams erupted from Hannah and the children as they looked toward the door. Hannah shivered as a blast of cold air blew over her, its fury causing the flames in the hearth to leap wildly, further frightening her.

Thomas gasped. There in the doorway, standing straight and tall, dressed in the full regalia typical of his tribe, stood the aging Gray Lock, the legendary, highly feared mighty chief of the Waranoke tribe. A bow was slung over his shoulder, and its quiver of sharp-tipped arrows hung down his back. His right hand gripped a wicked-looking, long-bladed hunting knife, which he pointed in the direction of Hannah and the children.

Hannah shooed the children behind her skirts and began to pray aloud. Meanwhile Thomas stepped forward in an attempt to lure Gray Lock away from his family.

The two men eyed one another, each sizing up his adversary. Gray Lock's dark, cruel-looking eyes surveyed Thomas and the others in the room while Thomas studied Gray Lock and silently contemplated the best way to rid his house of this dangerous visitor.

The unarmed Thomas took another defiant step forward and courageously confronted the Indian. "Leave my home now!" he demanded. "You are not welcome here. This is my home, and if you dare harm any member of my family, there will be many serious consequences."

Gray Lock seemed unmoved. He continued to eye Hannah and the children as if planning his next move. Then he focused his hostile gaze on Thomas for one last brief moment, and finally, to everyone's amazement and relief, turned and vanished through the front door.

Thomas slammed the door shut and quickly threw the bar. Then Hannah and the children unashamedly began to weep.

"Oh, Thomas," Hannah wailed. "We might have all been killed."

"Hush," he said lovingly, gathering his family into his arms to console them. "It's all over now. Gray Lock is gone. The Lord is with us. Thanks be to God."

After the incident, the story concludes, Gray Lock conferred with his tribesmen, bragging that he'd already had many opportunities to kill the Noble children. But as Boltwood noted in his *Genealogy*, "he [Gray Lock] wanted captives much more than he wanted scalps."[12]

Word spread quickly about the Nobles' terrifying encounter with the Indian chief. The Westfield settlers became more cautious and more protective of their families. After the episode with Gray Lock, Thomas kept his musket by his side wherever he went, but he never had occasion to use it on the Indian. Although Gray Lock was frequently seen in the Woronoco area, the chief never again returned to the Noble home. Nevertheless, several kidnappings by local Indians were reported during that time, with children the primary victims.

Some families moved to other parts of New England, where the Indians were known to be friendlier. In her popular book *The Courage of Sarah Noble,* Alice Dalgliesh tells of a distant cousin of Thomas's whose father, John Noble, was a guide and fur trapper. John eventually set up a homestead in Connecticut. He often left his eight-year-old daughter Sarah in the care of the local Indians while he was off working.

The Nobles of Westfield and the Clifford Noble Line of Descent

Westfield was permanently settled in 1666 and was officially granted the status of township in 1669. Thomas Noble rapidly became a significant pillar of his community and was elected constable and took the oath of allegiance in 1674. He took the oath of allegiance to his Majesty in 1678; joined the Westfield Church in February, 1681; and was admitted as a freeman in October 1861, providing him with full privileges of a citizen. At about that same time, he was named a Selectman and was thereafter considered one of the most powerful men in the town.[13]

Thomas and Hannah had made their permanent home in the new settlement and over the years they had ten children. The names of the people they married read like the history of early America. One of their sons was Matthew, who was born about 1668. From Matthew and his wife Hannah (Dewey), daughter of Thomas and Constant (Hawes) Dewey, whom he married on December 10, 1690, came the branch of the Thomas Noble family from which G. Clifford Noble was descended.[14]

Unfortunately, the town's records from the Revolutionary War period are not available. Accordingly, little is known about that period or about the time immediately preceding it, other than that the people who lived there were devoted to the cause of freedom and many faithful men, including several Nobles, joined the military and were recognized for their bravery.

3

Westfield as Home

Clifford's parents, James and Andelucia (Loomis) Noble.

Let us have faith that right makes might, and in that
faith let us to the end dare
to do our duty as we understand it.

—Abraham Lincoln (Cooper Union Speech)

◆   ◆   ◆

The roots that Clifford's parents put down in Westfield, Massachusetts, enabled him to grow up in a family and community that valued faith, morality, patriotism, and social responsibility. What we know about James and Andelucia Noble and the history of their time provides a key to Clifford's own character.

James Noble II, Clifford Noble's father, was born on June 25, 1833, in West Parish (now Mundale), Massachusetts.[1] He grew to manhood and married Andelucia Loomis, the slight but spirited daughter of Thomas and Julia (Shepard) Loomis, also of West Parish, on October 29, 1855.[2]

The new couple's first home in Westfield, where their first son, Fred Arthur, was born in 1859, was very old and in serious disrepair. So James and his neighbors held a home-razing celebration in preparation for the construction of the two buildings that would become the family's permanent farm home and barn at 118 Union Street.

The Nobles' new home resembled other homes in small New England towns during that period. It was a rectangular-shaped clapboard two-story with four small bedrooms upstairs and a large, open living area downstairs. The downstairs area featured an oversized, simple fireplace and a makeshift stove. With its chamber pots and outdoor privies, the house was hardly luxurious, but it was to become the Nobles' permanent home; one that the family cherished. The neighbors also built the Nobles a small barn in the rear of their property.

The construction of the new home took about ten days to complete from start to finish, with each man assigned a segment of the project according to his particular expertise. The workdays were long, but the women kept the men happy and motivated by serving them a tempting assortment of home-baked cakes and doughnuts, coffee, and fresh lemonade. Once the day's work was completed, the men gathered together to bandy stories before heading home to do the milking and other farm chores before dark.

When the new farm home stood proud and sturdy at the end of the final day's work, all the neighbors gathered to celebrate. The ladies wore long, colorful gingham skirts and cotton blousons, and the men were dressed in well-worn overalls, long-sleeved shirts, and farm hats. A few of the men brought their fiddles, and everyone joined in the dancing as the musicians strummed their lively renditions of the popular tunes of the day.

Despite the gaiety, the world beyond Westfield at that time was not quite so idyllic and jovial. James and Andelucia Noble began their married life during one of the darkest and most chaotic periods in American history.

In just a few short years, the United States would literally be split in two over controversies pertaining to slavery. While Northerners typically harbored antislavery sentiments, the Southern economy relied heavily upon slave labor. Slaves worked on the tobacco and cotton plantations in large numbers, and many Southerners were determined to keep it that way, believing that without slaves they would be unable to operate their plantations. Although some Northern farmers owned a few slaves, primarily using them in their businesses and homes, most did not. A major exception was New York—the major slave-holding city in the north. Slaves in New York were used to build roads, docks, the wall for which Wall Street was named, many of the more important buildings of the time, and the first English and Dutch churches.

In 1860, when the time came to elect a new president, the Southern states voted to leave the Union and establish their own confederacy if Abraham Lincoln was elected president. The forty-nine-year-old Lincoln was a successful lawyer who had been actively involved in state and national politics, but he was not the national figure that his opponent, Senator Stephen Douglas was. Douglas was one of the great debaters of his time. Lincoln, however, had been successful in engaging Douglas in a series of debates in which his eloquent attacks on slavery made him nationally well-known and popular among the Northerners.

Many of those who lived in the Northern states rallied around the gangly former Whig congressman who "had helped launch Illinois' new antislavery Republican Party"[3] and volunteered to help in his campaign.

Douglas ran on a platform of popular sovereignty—one that allowed settlers to make their own decisions about whether or not their state should retain slavery—a position that appealed to those who lived in the Southern states.

James and Andelucia worked tirelessly on Lincoln's presidential campaign. They distributed flyers and attended and hosted fundraising receptions. They also labored endlessly to get out the vote, even though Andelucia sorely lamented the fact that only men could vote. (It was not until August 26, 1920, with the passage of the Nineteenth Amendment, that women were granted the right to vote. Andelucia never had the opportunity to vote or to celebrate. She died earlier that same year.)

Lincoln was elected president in November 1860.The news of Lincoln's election was flashed by telegraph throughout the country. It sent shockwaves through the South, which felt its future was in serious jeopardy. By the time Lincoln took the oath of office on March 4, 1861, South Carolina had seceded from the Union, followed by six more "cotton states" including Georgia, Florida, Alabama, Mississippi, Louisiana, and Texas. This new Southern union, known as the

Confederacy, established its capital at Richmond, Virginia. Jefferson Davis was named president.

The Civil War

The first premonition of the Civil War appeared in the *Westfield News Letter* in early 1861. A January article reported on the sailing of a steamer from New York with twenty-five troops on board. They were headed for Charleston, South Carolina, to lend support to Major Robert Anderson, the Union officer who was in command of a small attachment of Union troops at Fort Sumter, located in the harbor of Charleston.[4]

In April of that year, the Confederates, with a force of several thousand men, fired on Fort Sumter. The fighting went on for some thirty hours until the fort caught fire and the greatly outnumbered Union soldiers were forced to surrender. This event not only precipitated the secession of Virginia, North Carolina, Tennessee, and Arkansas from the Union, bringing the number of seceding states to eleven, but it also marked the beginning of the Civil War.

The surrender of Fort Sumter stirred up the entire nation. President Lincoln took advantage of countless speaking opportunities to call for volunteers to defend the United States and save the Union. The response was immediate and overwhelming, and armies of volunteers enlisted in the Union's army.

The *Westfield News Letter* of April 24, 1861, featured many articles regarding the respective responses of various towns in Massachusetts to the president's appeal for its defense. Northampton, for example, voted to raise $25,000 to defend the Union and it formed two or three companies of volunteers to join the Union troops.[5]

The citizens of Westfield were equally supportive. They proudly displayed the American flag on their homes and businesses. Whenever a business raised a flag, that event was accompanied by appropriate public ceremonies that included patriotic speeches, and musical performances by the Westfield Brass Band.

In 1862, at a packed local town hall meeting, James Noble, his cousin, Reuben Noble and others were appointed by the meeting's moderator to a small committee of local citizens to raise $10,000. Those funds were to be appropriated by the town for the equipment and outfit of volunteers from Westfield, for the volunteer's pay, and for aid to their families during their absence.[6]

The committee was later asked to recruit seventy-five men and more if necessary in response to the president's call for 900,000 additional volunteers. The committee completed these assignments successfully. The volunteers they recruited became known as Company K, 10th Regiment Massachusetts Volunteers.[7] The men drilled in Springfield and left for Boston, later participating in the Battle of Gettysburg.

Although no Civil War battles were fought within Massachusetts itself, the state played a major role in the war. When President Lincoln called for troops, Massachusetts was quick to respond. Throughout the war Massachusetts secured both troops and money for the war effort and the state suffered more than its share of casualties.

Westfield, whose population totaled only about 5,000 residents at that time, sent more than 500 men to fight in the war. The community, with James leading still another fundraising effort, was also very generous in contributing funds for the bounties, or bonus payments that were used to entice men to enlist.

The local newspaper, the *Westfield News Letter*, carried daily war news columns that described in detail the outcomes of battles and the reports of local enlistees. The paper also published letters from local soldiers and ran recruitment ads. On January 7, 1864, one such ad called for "Veteran Volunteers to let Western Massachusetts respond to the President's call and be foremost in striking the final blow to the rebellion." The newspaper went on to report that "a $727 bounty was offered to all veterans who enlisted and a $427 bounty to all others."

Although James Noble did not enlist because of his age and family status, he and his wife were both actively involved in the local war effort. Andelucia kept busy stitching flags and regimental emblems. She and James also participated in Massachusetts's various antislavery activities. At the time, Massachusetts was leading an active abolitionist movement and many local citizens, including the Nobles, participated in a unique war effort designed to support the slaves' quest for freedom.

The Underground Railroad

Andelucia and James joined a secret network of sympathetic men and women who subjected themselves to considerable risk in order to help provide refuge ("safe houses"), food, and clothing for the runaway slaves. This network was known as the "Underground Railroad." James and Andelucia realized that they could be heavily fined for their activities, but they both remained fervently opposed to slavery and determined that the bounty hunters would not profit from the misfortune of others.

Most of the slaves whom James and Andelucia helped were routed through Massachusetts from the Virginia area. The frightened runaways were forced to travel hundreds of miles in the dark of night through desolate areas. But with the help of the Underground Railroad, many of these slaves were able to make their way north to freedom in Canada.

At that time, Springfield was the primary Underground Railroad center in Western Massachusetts. Many escaped slaves made their way up the Connecticut Valley by traveling from one safe house to another. Those who reached Springfield were sent to nearby Westfield. They stopped there for a day or two, where they were hidden in various places owned by local citizens.

Westfield residents provided the escaped slaves with money, food, and clothing. The Nobles recruited several sympathetic neighbors to help them prepare food, box up farm products, and clothing for the runaways. The safe houses in Westfield, though kept secret, were reportedly located on Main, Franklin, and School Streets, not far from where the Nobles lived. James and Andelucia maintained close but cautious communication with their Underground counterparts in Boston and the surrounding area so that they could be kept informed about the various needs of the slaves being routed through their region.

As an ardent and tireless abolitionist, Andelucia Noble vigorously supported the war effort. She often spoke at public gatherings, expressing her opposition to slavery and her support for President Lincoln. She was a passionate crusader who must have possessed amazing moral strength and courage. Those who knew her, or knew about her, described her as being both feminine and assertive and a very effective and persuasive advocate for the principles and morals she held dear.

Although Andelucia was also an outspoken supporter of temperance and women's suffrage, her life was centered in her faith and family. She cooked the family's meals and hand sewed, mended, and washed their clothes without help from any modern-day machines or conveniences. She was also a nurturing mother to her growing family and was the one who taught her children how to live and work in harmony with God.

On January 1, 1863, Lincoln issued his famous Emancipation Proclamation which declared an end to slavery and proclaimed freedom for nearly four million slaves in the Southern states. The Nobles rejoiced over the proclamation. It infused new spirit into the Union Army, whose courageous troops had been fighting to win back the seceded states and end slavery forever. But the Nobles knew that unless the war could be won, the Emancipation Proclamation would be worthless.

That summer, the Confederate leader, General Robert E. Lee, marched up the Shenandoah Valley and invaded the North. The Union forces, under General Meade, were ordered to use every means to stop Lee. The bloody battles that followed, ones that would decide the fate of the nation, began at the small town of

Gettysburg, Pennsylvania, on July 1, 1863. The battles raged for three days. Thousands of lives were lost. On July 3, approximately 15,000 Confederate soldiers, led by General George Pickett, made their last desperate charge against the Union forces but were repelled by a ferocious and bloody rifle and artillery encounter. More than half of the troops were killed or wounded. Lee finally retreated and withdrew his shattered army into Virginia. This was the turning point of the war. The Union cause was soon to be won.

The Nobles, who closely followed the local newspaper reports on the war and rejoiced over the victory at Gettysburg, soon found cause to celebrate once more. On January 7, 1864, amid the turmoil and uncertainty of the Civil War, their second son, Gilbert Clifford Noble, was born.

Aftermath of the War

The Civil War officially ended in April 1865, when General Robert E. Lee surrendered to General Ulysses S. Grant at Appomattox Court House near Richmond, Virginia. Later that year, the passage of the Thirteenth Amendment to the Constitution abolished slavery altogether.

The South now lay in ruins. Millions of people who had once lived in bondage emerged as free men and women, and the cotton and tobacco plantations lay deserted. The men who were once slaves, now called "freedmen," were given the right to vote. All the hard work that James and Andelucia and their friends had provided, played a defining role in this historic event.

James and Andelucia enthusiastically supported Lincoln for reelection. Lincoln campaigned on his plan for the reconstruction of the country and the restoration of each state to its original position in the Union. He was easily elected to a second term.

In his inaugural speech, President Lincoln pledged to "bind up the nation's wounds," but he never lived to do so. In the midst of the many celebrations held at the end of the Civil War, just five days after Lee's surrender on April 14, 1865, he was shot and killed while attending a performance at Ford's Theatre in Washington DC. The assassin was John Wilkes Booth, an actor, who was angry at the outcome of the war.

The news of the Lincoln's assassination was received in Westfield with great sadness. Village bells tolled, and an interdenominational church service was held at the First Congregational Church at noon on Wednesday, April 19, 1865. James and Andelucia attended, bringing along baby Clifford and six-year-old Fred Arthur. A few years later, the former Confederate states were readmitted to the Union.

On May 26, 1871, eight hundred Westfield citizens participated in the dedication of a monument; a granite pedestal surmounted by a soldier in bronze, that was erected at the foot of Court Street, southwest of the Green. The statue memorialized the heroic contributions of the Westfield men who lost their lives in defense of their country.[8]

James and Andelucia, now with three young children in tow, were among those who came to pay their respects and mourn with the families who had lost loved ones. On that day, many dynamic speakers recounted stories of terrible battles and the bravery of the Westfield recruits. Their horrific reports made a strong impression on seven-year-old Clifford Noble, who, through his parents, had developed a keen interest in the war. In fact, the Civil War would play a prominent role in some of Clifford's books, and Abraham Lincoln would remain his lifetime hero and subject of many of the stories that he later told his children.

The Death of Clifford's Father

When James Noble died suddenly in 1900, at the age of 67, "of acute congestion of the stomach and liver, complicated by heart trouble", the Westfield newspaper eulogized him as having been "one of the best known citizens of the town"…"a formidable local leader." According to his obituary, published in the *Westfield News* of March 1, 1900, James Noble was a "large-hearted man, ever ready to assist those in distress. He was a citizen of high ideals and not afraid to stand up for his own convictions. His voice was frequently heard in town meetings and public hearings, and, once he became interested in an issue, he put his whole soul into bringing about the desired end."

Following his funeral service at the Second Congregation Church, James Noble was buried in the Noble mausoleum in Westfield's Pine Hill Cemetery on West Silver Street. The mausoleum was a small, simple stone structure which he had commissioned, and one in which all of his immediate family members were later entombed, except for his son, Clifford. No doubt inspired by his father's effort, and determined to build something that would serve as the final resting place for his own large family, Clifford chose to build a much grander mausoleum at Kensico Cemetery in Valhalla, New York. Clifford's father never lived long enough to see his son's mausoleum but Clifford was convinced that his father probably would have been surprised at the size and ostentation of that structure—as he had always lived a very simple life.

In addition to serving on the board of directors of the Hamden National Bank in Westfield, James' obituary noted that he had devoted most of his life to supporting such causes as temperance, women's suffrage, improved public education, responsive and responsible government, and the abolition of slavery. His dedication to these issues made him an extremely popular and much-loved figure in his community.

It was in this environment of patriotism and a passionate commitment to the primary causes of the day that Clifford was born and raised. Clifford would later acknowledge those circumstances as having had a profound influence on the forging of his lifetime character.

James Noble's family mausoleum in Westfield, Massachusetts. The author visiting in 2004.

4

Birth and Early Years

Clifford Noble at age three, left, and age seven. (It is interesting to note that the photographer was likely the Nobles' favorite Westfield professional. In both photos, Clifford sits in the same tasseled chair.)

Life is a flame that is always burning itself out, but it catches fire again every time a child is born.

—George Bernard Shaw

"Whatever was that?" a frightened five-year-old Fred Arthur Noble asked his father as a shrill cry reverberated throughout the house. The cry intensified and repeated itself twice more.

Bright firelight flickered across the boy's small face as a bitterly cold January wind blustered against the eaves. The force of the gusts caused the wooden shutters to bang loudly against the side of the house, almost obscuring the sound that came from upstairs.

Though none knew it yet, the final days of the Civil War had begun to unfold like the bloodred petals of a monstrous rose. The date was January 7, 1864, just over a year from the day that Abraham Lincoln had delivered his historic Emancipation Proclamation and only fifteen months before he would be assassinated. It was also a date that would always have special significance for the Noble family.

James Noble stood and smiled broadly at Arthur. "Why, I believe that's the voice of our new baby," he said, beaming, as he lovingly patted his young son on the top of his head.

From the stairs above a happy voice called, "It's a boy! Another precious boy, Mr. Noble!" The midwife raced down a few steps, leaned over the stairwell and said, "He's a bit small, but he's certainly letting the whole world know he's arrived!"

"How is Andelucia?" James asked anxiously. He had expected his wife to have a long and difficult labor, and he was delighted to learn that this had not been the case.

"Mrs. Noble and the baby are doing just fine. If you'd like, you and Arthur can come upstairs now and see for yourselves."

James lifted Arthur into his arms and raced up the stairs.

Andelucia lay in her bed, propped up on several pillows, proudly cuddling her new infant son. James gave his wife a warm, approving embrace and then carefully picked up the whimpering infant and cradled him in his arms. "Arthur, come meet your new brother, Gilbert Clifford Noble," he said, smiling warmly.

More curious than excited, Arthur hastened to his father's side. "Hi, Gilbert Clifford," he whispered, carefully enunciating his new brother's name and looking a bit surprised at the small size of the wiggling infant. "I'm your big brother." Arthur gently patted the baby and tried without success to pick him up.

Andelucia laughed, while James said firmly, "I think we'd better let your mother hold Clifford for now. You'll get a turn soon enough."

That seemed to appease young Arthur. He remained quietly by his mother's side for the next two hours, completely engrossed in the antics of the new baby, until the new arrival finally fell asleep.

The perennial question about the origins of the name Gilbert Clifford remains unanswered. Because there were apparently no Gilberts or Cliffords in the immediate family, later Nobles have speculated that these names were most likely popular at that time and had simply been two of James and Andelucia's favorites. Whatever the case, G. Clifford, as he came to be known, was forever proud of his name, even though none of his own four sons inherited it.

Two more children were to be born into the James Noble family in the ensuing years. Howard Gustavo arrived in 1867, and Julia came in 1872. The Nobles also invited soft-spoken and self-reliant Alice Blakeslee, who was born in 1863 and lived on Russell Mountain, to come live with them.[1] Alice's parents were reportedly deceased, and her family members were considered unfit to have custody, although no written records have been found to prove this. Even though Alice was never officially adopted by the Nobles, she fitted into the family well and grew up right alongside the four Noble children. She eventually married Wolcott Daniels, a whip maker, in a small family wedding in the Nobles' home. The newlyweds set up housekeeping in a small home on West School Street, just a few short blocks from the Nobles' house.

Family Life in Westfield

Clifford Noble was born at a time when Westfield was still a small, highly rural farming community with a population of about 5,000. The town's long history included growing, curing, and manufacturing tobacco and tobacco products. Cigar manufacturing began in the area in the 1840s, and for many years Westfield was one of the primary tobacco centers of the Connecticut Valley, exporting cigars and tobacco products around the world.

Not only did James Noble have his hand in the tobacco business (he grew and cured tobacco in his backyard until his tobacco barn mysteriously burned down), but he was also an accomplished whip maker. He was thought to be one of the principals of a large local manufacturing company that produced handmade whips and lashes for the horse and buggy trade and sold them for anywhere from five cents to fifty cents apiece.[2] By 1855, whip-making had become mechanized and by the end of the nineteenth century, the whip-making industry in Westfield produced over ninety-five percent of the world's whips, earning the town the title of "The Whip City of the World."[3] Although James's company expanded, he opted to reduce his ownership in the business, and eventually sold all of his stock in order to devote his full time and attention to farming.

Despite his participation in the whip-making and tobacco businesses, James was primarily a small farmer, as were most residents of Westfield. This was the business James knew and loved. With the help of his sons as they grew older, he plowed and planted such crops as sugar beets (for cattle feed), corn, and potatoes.

He weeded, cultivated, and harvested his bounty in the fall, much as Thomas Noble had done generations earlier.

Summer was reserved for livestock butchering—a job Clifford abhorred, as he could never resist becoming attached to the farm animals. It was this bloody, stomach-wrenching chore, which he reluctantly helped his father with, which convinced Clifford that farming was not the vocation he'd choose to pursue.

In addition to his other interests, James also invested in a cattle ranch in Colorado with Dr. H. M. Miller, a local dentist whose brick home stood at the intersection of Meadow and Elm Streets in Westfield. Although the ranch was projected to be a highly profitable investment, the men's dreams of great wealth vanished after three short years when a devastating snowstorm buried the ranch's winter forage and most of the cattle starved to death.[4]

James learned a lesson the hard way, and he later preached it to his sons: "Speculating in areas about which you know nothing is generally unwise." Subsequently he assured his family that he'd concentrate on farming—the business he knew best—a lesson Clifford would take to heart and follow later in life.

Like her husband, Andelucia played a major role in instilling sound values and high ideals in her children. Her job was to maintain the household, which she did in part by canning and preserving the fruits and vegetables harvested on the farm, but she was also equally responsible for the care and nurturing of her children.

Andelucia spent many hours helping her children with their schoolwork and reading them *Aesop's Fables* and stories from the Bible. She also told them tales about the Civil War and Abraham Lincoln, and she shared emotionally charged true stories about several individuals who had been sold as slaves. Many of these stories had been told to her by the very slaves she had helped, so she was able to describe the horror of their lives in vivid terms. Her stories underscored the inhumanity of the slave trade, the separation of children from their family and husband from wife, the merciless beatings that some slaves endured for the slightest of transgressions, and other graphic examples of their oppression and denial of any rights. Her stories were real and terrifying and graphically taught her children right from wrong.

Clifford thrived on the storytelling. Storytelling set Clifford's moral compass at an early age and he was to use this technique to teach values to his own children during their formative years.

It was also his mother who instilled in him his love of reading, appreciation for books, and fascination with history. Some of the books he later wrote and published contained stories that his mother had read to him when he was a child.

School Days

School and the town's Universalist Church took top priority in the Noble household, and attendance and active participation at both were a given.

Located some distance from the street, the Noble children's one-story wooden schoolhouse is now a residence on Springvale Avenue.[5] It stood beneath the partial shade of a glorious old maple tree whose leaves put on an awe-inspiring show of color every fall to welcome students back to class. It was in this school that Clifford's favorite teachers tolerated his boyish antics, mentored him, inspired him to academic excellence, and gave him his solid educational foundation.

Clifford, right, and his older brother, Arthur; high school wrestlers—1870s.

Maintaining order and discipline at the school was sometimes a problem, and the town's only police officer, George Miner, was often called in to straighten things out. Although Clifford did have a prankster's reputation, and although he undoubtedly did participate in his share of misbehavior, he was never a serious behavior problem at school. In fact, he frequently attempted to dissuade some of his friends from causing trouble.

After completing his studies at that school, Clifford entered "B" Class in the much larger Davis School on Bartlett Street, where he became known for his exemplary deportment and high academic standing.

Clifford was also active in the school's modest athletic program and worked out in the gymnasium to stay fit. He and his older brother, Arthur, participated on the school's wrestling team. They were both tough competitors. The two brothers also enjoyed baseball and played a variety of the same key positions, including pitcher and shortstop, on the school's baseball team. Public school athletics and facilities were limited, but the brothers enjoyed their participation, their opportunities to compete, and the warm and approving response they received from their parents and from the friends and neighbors who regularly attended their athletic events.

Dreams of Becoming a Preacher

On weekends and evenings, the Davis School doubled as a meeting place for religious revivals conducted by Peter Culins, a woodworker, who preached there or at the Gem Roller Skating Rink in the rear of the Lane and Loomis block behind 124–128 Elm Street.[6] Clifford attended the revivals whenever he could, without his parents' knowledge or permission. He didn't tell them what he was doing because he knew that they would not approve of this nontraditional practice of religion. But he loved the evangelistic fervor of the services and the opportunity to listen to scripture readings and participate in the simple musical ministry of the service.

Revivals were very popular in Westfield at that time, and they attracted people of all ages. Upwards of seventy-five to one hundred people regularly attended. The congregants sat in very uncomfortable straight-backed wooden fold-up chairs, intent upon listening to Preacher Culins's gospel message.

Clifford was the ideal addition to those revivals, and Preacher Culins eagerly accepted the offer of his musical talent. Clifford sang beautifully. His melodious tenor voice harmonized easily with the voices of the congregation, and he would often accompany himself on the piano or banjo, both of which he played remarkably well. Although he had never taken any formal music lessons, he had learned to play by ear, practicing on the pianos at his school and church and wherever else he could find an instrument.

The crowd loved Clifford's music, so Mr. Culins decided to let him try his hand at preaching once in awhile, an assignment that Clifford had coveted. He was also called upon to pass the collection basket. Culins knew that Clifford's youthful charm and appeal would increase contributions, and Clifford never disappointed him.

Despite his love of the revival services, Clifford knew that he was taking a serious risk by attending. Should his parents discover his whereabouts, he'd be in serious trouble. And one night, as luck would have it, his father appeared unexpectedly at the revival.

Clifford had just laid aside his banjo and was walking to the podium to preach when he heard a loud commotion in the back of the room. When he looked back, he was appalled to see his father standing there. James Noble's arms were crossed over his chest, and his frightening facial expression offered clear evidence of what he was thinking.

"Clifford!" he shouted in a voice so loud it attracted the attention of all those in attendance.

The room hushed.

"Clifford, come here! Immediately. Do these good people know you're only fourteen years old? That's way too young to be preaching the gospel at this time of night. Besides, you're not at all that knowledgeable about scripture. You should be home doing your homework like your brothers and sister."

Clifford had been taken by complete surprise and was mortified by his father's angry outburst. He wasn't sure what to do next. He glanced around the room trying to interpret the reaction of his audience. The very people he thought had become his devoted followers now wore amused smiles on their faces. Some of the women even tried to hide their laughter behind their lace hankies.

Clifford was so humiliated that he couldn't even talk. He slowly picked up his banjo and obediently left the arena, following closely behind his father with not so much as a glance back at the congregation.

At home that evening, after his mother and father had both soundly scolded him in front of his wide-eyed siblings, Clifford's father told him to fetch a branch from a tree in the yard which he used for the traditional spanking when his children misbehaved. It came as no surprise to anyone in the family that after that sound spanking, young G. Clifford Noble's grandiose ideas of becoming a famous preacher ended.

Finding Jobs at Church

The Noble family regularly attended the Universalist Church, where the Reverend D. H. Plumb served as pastor. The church building was a converted dwelling located on the north side of Chapel Street, just a few short blocks from Union Street. Relieved that Clifford was no longer yearning to participate in the revivals, his parents urged him to take a more active role in their church. The congregation was a committed and active one, and the children of the parishioners were all encouraged to participate in the various church ministries.

One day the Rev. Plumb announced that he needed some help. Addressing the many children sitting in the pews beside their parents, he asked, "Do I have anyone in my congregation who would like to volunteer their time for the Lord's work? Our music ministry is a very important part of our service, and our organist needs some young people to help pump the bellows."

Clifford poked Howard in the ribs. "Hey, that's a good job for you," he whispered. "I don't know what you'd have to do, but it does sound interesting."

But a visibly annoyed Howard rebelled—not so much because he was tired of being volunteered by his older brother, but because he didn't want to be the *only* volunteer.

"I'll do it if you will," Howard countered. After thinking about it and talking quietly together, the boys shook hands in agreement. After the service ended, they sought out the organist to offer their help.

As the Rev. Plumb had suggested, the job entailed sharing the duty of pumping the organ's bellows during the church services. In an area beneath the organ, a couple of bellows provided the organ's wind supply. Inflating the bellows required pumping on a pedal lever. The boys found the job to be a monotonous and tiring one. But Howard reminded Clifford in a barely audible whisper, as they worked the bellows that first Sunday, "This isn't as bad as having to sit with everybody else in church on those hard wooden pews. Then we'd really have to pay attention to the daily lesson and a long sermon. Besides, if we stay busy and smile a lot, that old organist is bound to give us a reward. And best of all, Mother and Father are going to be so happy that we're doing our part for the Lord."

Clifford had to admit that Howard's reasoning was sound. The job proved to be financially and personally rewarding for the boys, and their unwitting parents were proud indeed.

Fighting Gamecocks

Union Street and the neighborhood immediately surrounding that area were home to many interesting people, one of whom was Lewis Hanchett. A whip maker by trade, Hanchett also raised dogs and boarded fighting gamecocks, which he kept in fifteen individual coops he had built especially for the prized birds. The cocks were owned by a group of men headed by Charles Foster, who owned the Foster House hotel on North Elm Street.[7]

One day while Hanchett was out of town, Clifford, Howard, and Hanchett's mischievous son Fred released a couple of the birds into the Hanchett's fenced backyard with the intention of staging a private afternoon cockfight. Each boy was anxious to determine which bird would prove best in battle. They placed imaginary wagers and prepared to root for their favorite competitor.

As the birds warily approached each other, Howard's enthusiasm turned to fear. "Clifford!" he cried. "That big one of mine looks like he's going to kill your bird. Do something!" They weren't at all prepared for the intense and bloody battle apparently about to begin.

The battle-ready birds stretched out their ferocious-looking, overly sharp spurs, ruffled their dark feathers, and methodically moved closer to one another. Howard was terrified. And Fred, knowing the value of these birds and acutely aware of what was about to happen, wisely decided that things had gone far enough.

"Fellows," he said firmly, "we have to stop this now. These birds have been in their cages far too long, and they appear more than ready to stage a serious fight. When I separate them, I want you to use these sticks to get them back into their cages before they kill one another."

Clifford readily agreed and quickly grabbed one of the sticks that Fred had picked up off the ground. He cautiously prodded the pugnacious birds back into their coops. When the birds were secured, the relieved boys told one another that they'd never attempt to stage another cockfight. The risks and possible consequences were far higher than they had imagined.

It's doubtful that any of the boys, particularly the Noble boys, realized at the time how cruel and brutal a cockfight could be. And Clifford couldn't help but recall the lesson his father had taught him the time they'd lost the cattle ranch in Colorado. It had to do with never getting involved in something he knew little or nothing about.

Fortunately for the boys, neither Mr. Hanchett nor Mr. Foster ever discovered that their expensive, highly prized, battle-ready gamecocks, publicly advertised as never having fought before, had almost become veterans of the sport.

The Union Street Improvement Society

When the Noble children were still relatively young, Howard reported in his paper, "A Trip Down Union Street", that their parents were asked to organize the Union Street Improvement Society. The group met in the different homes every two or three weeks. Its purpose was to organize and implement projects and activities that would improve the neighborhood. The men were responsible for carrying out the plans that the Society approved, such as road grading, rebuilding sidewalks, buying and setting up kerosene lamps, and paying the lamp lighter.[8]

Meetings were rotated among the members' homes, with the woman of the home serving as hostess. She was responsible for providing refreshments—usually lemonade and freshly baked pastries—and some form of simple entertainment.

Clifford looked forward to these meetings, especially those hosted by his parents, because they gave him the chance to perform in front of an appreciative, if not merely a polite, audience. In time, he became quite well-known for his clever recitations and musical abilities. He played the piano and the banjo, and his remarkably mellow tenor voice placed him in great demand among the hosts of Society meetings.

The neighbors all loved Clifford's spontaneity and youthful energy. Little did they know that whenever he or Howard were invited to recite, they would spend hours practicing in the family's cow barn, standing on a pile of manure while James Noble milked the cows nearby and critiqued their performance. But the stench of the manure in the "practice hall" didn't seem to discourage either of the boys from learning their performance pieces.

Clifford borrowed most of his pieces from his tattered schoolbooks. One of his favorite poems from Charles Sanders' *Union Reader (1801)* was titled, "The Boy and His Dog Rover," which Clifford acted out dramatically as he recited the lines.

Clifford was often known to be a bit unpredictable with his presentations and frequently provided some theatrical asides, but his audience was always very receptive to whatever he offered, and he thrived on the thunderous applause he generally received.

In fact, Clifford was invited to perform so often at the Society meetings that he became quite smug about his talent, much to the disgust of his brothers. He had even convinced himself that he would one day be a great New York actor or orator—a prospect he found enormously intriguing. That dream was a throwback, perhaps, to his earlier failed plans of becoming a preacher.

Several years later while he was at Harvard, Clifford confessed his secret ambition to close friends. He admitted that his oratorical skills were probably better suited for college debates than for the stages of New York. And it should not have come as a surprise to anyone, especially not to his family, that no one, not even his closest friends, disagreed.

5

Dreams of College

Clifford with his siblings. Pictured left to right are Arthur (sitting), Howard (standing), Julia, and Clifford.

There comes that mysterious meeting in life when someone acknowledges who we are and what we can be, igniting the circuits of our highest potential.

—Rusty Berkus
—Bobbi Sims, *Don't Let 'em Crumble Your Cookies*

During Clifford Noble's formative years, there were no amusements such as video games, television, or computers that children enjoy today. Clifford and his siblings had to depend upon themselves for fun. In the small farming communities like Westfield, that were a long way from the larger urban areas that offered more varied entertainment, families were important social units.

The Noble children often gathered in the evenings for prayers, family games, and conversation after they completed school assignments, studying, and other homework. House rules dictated that all homework be done first, and the children knew that if they chose to ignore these rules, they jeopardized their free time privileges. But their time together was sacred. Family members shared joy-filled hours and love as well as activities and academic discussions that unified them and brought the Noble family members closer together.

Clifford enjoyed school, and he thrilled to the satisfaction that he derived from learning new things. He was a good student, and because reading was his favorite pastime, he often spent his free time visiting the Westfield Athenaeum, the city's unpretentious one-room public library.[1] The Athenaeum stood on Main Street, a handsome brick building with brownstone trimmings. The library not only provided Clifford with an unlimited selection of good books, it also offered him a welcome respite from work on the farm.

Clifford loved a good adventure story, but biographies of interesting people were his favorites. He also read the Bible in its entirety and worked his way through Shakespeare, John Bunyan's *Pilgrim's Progress*, Walt Whitman's *Leaves of Grass*, and Parson Weems's *The Life of George Washington*.

Several of his teachers recognized his deep curiosity and excellent reading skills, and encouraged him to read books beyond his expected reading level. They spent much time outside of regular school hours helping to build his vocabulary and teaching him how to quickly grasp the central theme of a text. Clifford not only listened to their sage advice, but faithfully practiced what he learned. When he was in secondary school, despite his popularity, he rarely dated or socialized. He preferred to go straight home after school to complete his homework so that he'd have ample time to read.

Learning had become Clifford's passion. He was curious about the world and about the people who had made a difference in it. By the time he reached the end of his third year in high school, he had one all-consuming dream: to go to college so that he could learn more and further his education.

Although only Clifford's father, James, a graduate of Wilbraham Academy, had been educated beyond the local public schools, both of Clifford's parents regularly preached the importance of having a good education. So Clifford was surprised when he learned that they did not support his interest in attending college. He avoided discussing the subject with them, hoping that they would eventually change their minds.

One evening at dinner, Clifford's father turned to him and said bluntly, "Clifford, I know you're bound to be disappointed over what I'm about to say, but your mother and I strongly oppose your thoughts of going to college."

"What?" Clifford asked, pretending not to hear what his father had said. "What did you say?" he asked again, hoping that perhaps he'd misinterpreted his father's comment.

"Son," Clifford's father replied, "your mother and I know that your heart is set on attending college, but frankly, we both feel that putting you through college would be a waste of your time and our money."

"But why?" Clifford asked, not fully understanding what his father was saying. "Won't you please speak to some of my teachers before you make your final decision? They've told me that I would make an excellent candidate for Harvard, and they want me to apply to both Harvard College and Harvard Medical School. And that's what I'd really like to do."

Then Clifford's mother spoke for the first time. "It isn't that we want to dash your dreams, my dear Clifford. We're very proud of you and very pleased that you've worked so hard throughout your years in school. We've even admired your many profitable business ventures. But we've become dependent upon your help on the farm and, quite frankly, we had hoped you would make a career of farming. Farming is what all your forebears have pursued, and we just don't understand why you don't want to follow in their footsteps."

Clifford found himself at an uncharacteristic loss for words. He could think of no plausible argument that might persuade his parents to change their minds, but he made one last attempt anyway.

"Won't you at least give this a little more thought before you make a final decision?" he pleaded tearfully. "Both of you are usually very fair-minded and willing to consider all sides of an issue. And this matter is so important to me that it should *not* be an exception. I have prayed about this, and I hope that both of you have, too."

James and Andelucia exchanged a guarded but sympathetic look but did not respond. The seconds of silence that followed seemed like hours to the anxious Clifford. Finally, after a brief, almost inaudible exchange of words with Andelucia, Clifford's father spoke. "All right, Clifford. Your mother and I *will* speak to your teachers, but we are not guaranteeing anything. Is that understood?"

"Yes, sir."

Then Clifford quickly excused himself from the table before his parents could reconsider their decision.

It is unclear exactly how Clifford's teachers finally managed to convince James and Andelucia to allow Clifford to apply to Harvard. Perhaps Clifford's prayerful longing got the best of them. But eventually they did agree, and once that decision was made, they never wavered. They wholeheartedly supported their gifted son's dream of going to college.

Application for Admission to Harvard

To help Clifford prepare for the challenging Harvard entrance exams, Clifford's teachers volunteered to spend extra time with him reviewing the topics the examinations would likely cover. Clifford had never seriously contemplated a medical career, but to pacify those selfless mentors who had invested considerable time and effort in his education, he applied to both Harvard College and Harvard Medical School. He was able to take the proctored entrance examinations for both schools in Westfield.

To everyone's surprise and relief, Clifford easily passed the entrance examinations. But Clifford soon learned that the exams represented only half of the entrance requirements. He would also have to endure an arduous personal grilling by the college president and various faculty members at Harvard College in late spring. Students who had already been through the ordeal warned Clifford that the interview would be far more challenging and demanding than the entrance examination.

That thought wasn't too comforting to Clifford the morning he climbed into the rear seat of the family's horse-drawn buggy for the drive to Cambridge for his interviews.

"You look quite handsome today, Clifford," Andelucia said, watching her son nervously adjust his wool cap and brush a speck of lint from one sleeve of his stylish navy blue pea jacket. "But I wish you wouldn't worry so. You'll do just fine."

The trip to Cambridge was stressful for the entire family. There was very little conversation among the passengers. Clifford found it difficult to pay attention to the beautiful New England countryside and its many colorful wildflowers. This was unusual for him; he was normally so outspoken about the beauty of nature and his parents were reluctant to ask him any questions.

Clifford's thoughts were consumed with the questions he kept asking himself. *What if my interview doesn't go well, and they reject me? What if I have to return to the farm?* This was a prospect his intellectually curious mind and fiery ambition simply could not abide. Clifford tried to divert his attention to other matters, but he found his thoughts returning again and again to the pending interviews.

He was thankful that he had taken great pains with his appearance that morning. The image that had stared back at him from the dresser mirror in his bedroom earlier that day had shown a clean-shaven eighteen-year-old of medium build who stood about five feet ten inches tall. With his tawny colored hair, twinkling blue eyes, and fine chiseled features, Clifford was a rather handsome young man.

He was even a bit amused by the thought that he might actually resemble the aristocratic, suave-looking Harvard students he had heard so much about—those young men who had graduated from popular preparatory schools in New England. That thought, coupled with the trendy new college clothes that his parents had purchased for him—especially for his interview, helped Clifford stem his apprehension and restore his waning self-confidence.

Although he had thought of practically nothing else for weeks, Clifford was not prepared for the scene that greeted him during his first visit to Harvard. The school was "nestled among stately elms and oaks, the Charles River gurgling past on one side and rustic Cambridge lying remote on another flank."[1]

The college and Harvard Yard was an imposing sight, with its ivy covered buildings, gravel walks and highly manicured lawns, but one which young Clifford found a bit overwhelming. That same feeling would be echoed a half century later by the school's twenty-second president, Abbot Lawrence Lowell, who wrote in the *History and Traditions of Harvard College* that "the entering Freshman will wander through the trim formality of the Harvard Yard without sensing the warm background of traditions formed during the three hundred years of its existence, However, acquaintances with it, as many generations of undergraduates have discovered, soon overcome the initial impression of austerity, and in the end—the Yard takes a foremost place in one's affections for Harvard."[2]

As soon as Clifford's father brought his buggy to a halt and secured the horses at the Johnson Gate, the main entrance to Harvard Yard, a somewhat reluctant Clifford bounded from the buggy and ran to the railings that surrounded the Yard to peer through, pointing out many of the various college landmarks to his parents that he had read about before making the trip.

"Well, Clifford, what do you think?" James asked. "Is it everything you had hoped for?"

"I can't believe I'm actually here," Clifford replied in hushed amazement. "It's even more imposing than I imagined."

They entered the Yard through the gate, and James stopped briefly to check his pocket watch. "We're just in time for the interview," he said, then looked around. "But I have no idea where you're to go."

Just then a well-dressed, rather mature-looking student, whom Clifford guessed to be an upperclassman, approached them. "Welcome to Harvard," he said. He introduced himself, then added, "I'm a senior this year, and I have been given the happy assignment of welcoming prospective new students. May I be of some assistance? You all seem a bit lost."

When Clifford explained why he was there, the older student volunteered to escort him to the administrative area where the college president, Charles William Eliot, maintained an office. In no time at all, the foursome reached the appropriate building.

"Well, I guess this is it," James said, patting Clifford's shoulder. "You're on your own now, Son. We'll wait for you right here. And we do both wish you good luck." Then he gave the youngster a manly embrace.

Andelucia gave her embarrassed son a parting kiss on the cheek. "Just be yourself," she wisely advised, and with that, Clifford followed his escort to the interview room adjacent to the president's office.

The Interview

At first glance, the dark-paneled interview room, with its polished, formal furniture, appeared rather foreboding, although Clifford couldn't decide whether it was the décor or his anxiety that made things seem that way. In the center of the room, a small group of men sat around a large round table. Clifford was still feeling quite nervous when one of the men stood, smiled warmly, and extended his hand.

The man was a well-built, aristocratic-looking individual in his late forties. He had well-defined facial features, fashionable wire-framed eyeglasses, a cropped hairstyle, and distinctive bushy sideburns.

Clifford stepped forward and shook the man's hand.

"I'm President Eliot," his host said warmly, "and I assume you are Gilbert Clifford Noble?"

"Yes, sir. But please just call me Clifford," a subdued Clifford responded, overwhelmed by being in the presence of the popular college president, whom he had read so much about.

President Eliot introduced Clifford to the rest of the men, all faculty members, explaining that everyone in the room was thoroughly familiar with Clifford's background and his fine academic capabilities.

"So," the president said, "we'll be spending our time today just getting to know you. We're going to try to make this meeting very informal, and we hope you'll feel free to answer our questions honestly and that *you* will ask us any questions that you might have."

Everyone seemed kind and friendly—not the least bit intimidating or demanding, as Clifford had been led to expect. They shook his hand and invited him to join them at the table.

"All right, Clifford," President Eliot began, "why don't you start by telling us why you decided to apply to Harvard."

Clifford glanced around the table, relieved that he'd been given an easy first question. This was to be an interview that he would long remember, one that he would recall in great detail when later encouraging two of his own sons to apply to Harvard.

"Harvard was my first and only choice," he began. "I considered no other colleges. It's close enough to home to allow my parents and family to visit once in a while, but more importantly, as you well know, Harvard is widely recognized as the premier school in the country. I've come to understand that it has no equal in its ability to educate young men like me and that it is known for helping its graduates achieve their dreams."

President Eliot smiled. "What *are your* dreams, Clifford?" he asked with sincere interest.

Clifford paused a moment to gather his thoughts, then said, "Well, sir, to be honest, I'm not altogether sure yet. But I do know that I'm just not cut out to be a farmer like my father and generations of Nobles before me. I want a new experience and a profitable and interesting career in a more intellectually stimulating environment."

Clifford stopped a moment before continuing. "Of course, I realize that farming is an important vocation. The nation certainly needs farmers. But my interests lie in the business world. I've watched my father farm through good times and bad and it concerns me that he has very little control over how well he does. His success depends largely upon the weather and the market."

Clifford looked at his interviewers, hoping they wouldn't feel he was trying to disparage farmers. But they all nodded their support and urged him to continue.

"I love books," he went on. "Reading is my passion. So after graduation, maybe I'll pursue some sort of job in the book industry. Someday I'd like to own my own company. That's always been a dream of mine. But for now, I am only sure of one thing: as soon as I graduate, I want to move to New York City. I have never been there; I've just read about it. I'm probably not prepared for the challenges that the big city offers, but I am confident that after four years at Harvard, I should be ready. And I am really looking forward to that move."

Clifford took a few deep breaths and cleared his throat, hoping that his nervousness wasn't too noticeable. "I can assure all of you," he said with all the conviction he could muster up, "that if I am accepted at Harvard, I will study hard. I hope to make each of you very proud some day."

Clifford settled back in his chair and waited for more questions, but none came. Instead, the group openly discussed his academic record, only conferring with him when they had questions about his grades or the subjects he had studied. After thirty minutes or so, President Eliot stood, thanked Clifford for sharing his ideas, and announced that the interview was over.

The faculty members rose from their chairs and shook hands with Clifford, who was a bit surprised by the brevity of the encounter. He was worried that he might have been too lacking in substantive answers to their queries or too self-assured during the interview. The worried look on his face must have given him away.

"Don't look so concerned," the faculty member next to him said reassuringly, patting him on the shoulder. "No need for that."

"You make an excellent candidate for the next freshman class," another interviewer added, warmly shaking his hand.

Finally, a smiling President Eliot approached him. "That's right, Clifford. We're all confident that you're smart enough and determined enough to do well at Harvard. And I think I speak for all of us when I tell you that we have all been impressed by you today. We look forward to having you at Harvard."

The favorable comments, especially those offered by the Harvard president, took Clifford by complete surprise and left the young college applicant in high spirits. As he left the room, he felt very confident about his future. He quickly located his anxious parents and began to tell them all about the people he'd met and everything they'd told him.

How different he seems from the somber young man who accompanied us on the ride to Cambridge earlier today, thought his mother. As the Nobles climbed into the buggy for their trip home, James encouraged Clifford to tell them all about his interview, which an exuberant and very loquacious Clifford happily did, the *entire* way home.

Acceptance

Clifford spent the next few trying days wavering between hope and despair as he waited to officially hear whether or not he had been admitted to Harvard. When the envelope containing the news of his acceptance into the Class of 1886 finally arrived, he realized that his instincts had been correct and that he'd worried needlessly. The truth was, as he later learned from faculty members who had been present the day of his interview, that he had charmed his interviewers with his candor, sincerity, and warm personality.

As he read and reread his acceptance letter, Clifford could hardly believe that he'd been accepted at *both* Harvard College and Harvard Medical School. His parents left the decision of which school to attend totally up to him. He took little time choosing Harvard College and promptly sent a handwritten note to President Eliot accepting the invitation and thanking him for the opportunity.

Eager to share his good news, Clifford ran to the schoolhouse to find his favorite teacher.

"Did you ever think that I'd be attending Harvard College?" he said to her. "I can hardly believe my good fortune. As you no doubt know, Harvard College is the oldest institution of higher learning in the country. The thought of eight signers of the Declaration of Independence having graduated from Harvard, as well as President Lincoln's son and several presidents of the United States, is a bit much for me to absorb. That's quite an impressive group of scholars, and I have to wonder if I'll be able to live up to that tradition."

Clifford's teacher smiled, reassured her visitor and encouraged him to continue.

"Well," Clifford said, "I have no idea what my future will bring, but I am confident that if I work hard enough, I can do most anything I set my mind to.

"You know, it's a funny thing. Most of what I've learned about life so far, I have learned on the farm. There are lots of similarities between farming and life in general. I have discovered that if you want to grow quality products, you begin by planting healthy seed in good soil, water and nurture it, keep the weeds and destructive elements from taking over, and then harvest it when it's ready.

"Well, that reminds me of *me*. Fortunately, I have been blessed with a solid foundation, and I've been provided with more than my share of protective care and nurturing, thanks to my parents and to teachers like you. And with a Harvard education, I should be more than ready for whatever life has to offer."

Clifford's confidante hugged him and smiled approvingly. "We all love your positive attitude, Clifford," she said tearfully, "and we will all certainly miss you."

After promising to remain in touch, Clifford left for home to prepare for the next phase of his life.

6

Harvard College

Clifford Noble, Harvard College, 1882

*"So...be your name Buxbaum or Bixby
or Bray Or Mordecai Ali Van Allen O'Shea,
You're off to Great Places! Today is your day!
Your mountain is waiting. So...get on your way."*

—Dr. Seuss, *Oh, The Places You'll Go!*

◆   ◆   ◆

When a young man goes off to college, it's often a time of mixed emotions for his family, his friends, and indeed, for the prospective student himself. Clifford's parents, considering their early misgivings about college, must have followed his progress intently, treasuring every word in his letters from Harvard and eagerly awaiting his next visit home. But Clifford adapted well to the college routine and seized every opportunity to further his quest for knowledge.

In the fall of 1882, at eighteen years of age, Gilbert Clifford Noble, the young farm boy from Westfield, Massachusetts, began his freshman year at Harvard College.

It was a glorious time to be in Cambridge and especially to be at Harvard College.

It was a picturesque setting and one that heightened Clifford's enthusiasm. The many trees on campus, in the early stages of their annual flamboyant and colorful leaf display, lined the campus. It was a reminder of home but far more dazzling, almost as if it had been especially staged to welcome and celebrate the arrival of the impressionable young Clifford.

Wholesome-looking young scholars were everywhere, strolling through campus in small groups or individually, enjoying the invigorating, crisp fall air. *Any of them,* thought Clifford, *would make wonderful representatives of America's finest school.*

College Experiences

Harvard was, and continues to be, a bastion of learning and one of the most highly regarded New England institutions. Clifford entered the college at a time when the school was in the midst of great academic and organizational changes. Its aristocratic European tradition of compulsory classical studies, regardless of individual interests, was no longer the order of the day.

In 1869, the college elected thirty-five-year-old Charles William Eliot, Class of '53, to undertake the controversial and challenging job of reforming and reshaping the curriculum of Harvard College and Harvard Medical and Law Schools.[1] Eliot was a strong proponent of the elective system; one in which Harvard students were given a choice of more than 450 course offerings. Eliot wanted each student's curriculum to be tailor-made to that student's interests and abilities.

As Abbott Lowell wrote in *The History and Traditions of Harvard College*:

> The idea of turning out a uniform Harvard product was abhorrent to him and he (President Eliot) preferred that some should be hurt by too much liberty, rather than risk robbing Harvard and the world of another Emerson or Thoreau, through a moulding process.[2]

In his inaugural address in which he touted his new elective system, President Eliot said, "The elective system fosters scholarship because it gives free play to natural preferences and inborn aptitudes, makes possible enthusiasm for a chosen work and relieves the professor...of the presence of a body of students who are compelled to an unwelcome task."[3]

Previous presidents had attempted some reforms, but their efforts had not been successful.

Had it not been for Eliot's often-controversial changes, Clifford Noble's future might have been quite different. He was definitely at Harvard at the right time in his life, and at the right time in Harvard's history.

During his administration Eliot also encouraged the formation of a more diverse, more socially conscious student body, but one in which social class distinction still prevailed. Harvard College had a history of attracting the sons of some of the country's wealthiest and most notable families, including men such as Henry Adams, William Randolph Hearst, and Theodore Roosevelt. But the college's new recognition of the sons of the less affluent provided Clifford with opportunities that would not have otherwise been available.

To support his philosophy, President Eliot argued vehemently against a proposal by the school's Overseers Committee to increase tuition by 50 percent. Eliot was concerned that the higher tuition would decrease the number of students from public schools at Harvard that comprised less than 30 percent of the student body at that time. Eliot believed that those of limited means constituted "the very best part of Harvard College." "Eliot prevailed, and the existing tuition of $150 per year was sustained until 1916."[4] That decision alone enabled Clifford to remain at college. Had it been otherwise, he was quite certain that his parents would have called him back home to a life on the farm.

In his book, *John Adams—A Life*, John Ferling noted that "The young men who attended Harvard at the time were above average students with a recognizable commonality. Most of them came from New England and the Middle Atlantic states, with the greatest number coming from Massachusetts. Most of these students were considered to be intellectually gifted, were primarily drawn from the middle and upper social classes and had been educated at some of New England's most prestigious private preparatory schools."[5]

Despite or perhaps because of Clifford's lower middle class and public school background, he found Harvard to be a stimulating and exciting place. Clifford was quickly recognized for his strong work ethic, excellent vocabulary, impressive scholastic skills, and his sensible and substantive thought and he had little difficulty becoming assimilated into the Harvard culture. He thrived at college and enjoyed the friendships he made with young men who shared his same interests.

No formal transcripts of Clifford's course work or academic performance at Harvard exists. But the college records that are available suggest that he was able to maintain high grades, largely through the encouragement of his two favorite (and very popular) faculty members, Professors Goodale and Nathaniel Southgate Shaler. Among the courses Clifford is known to have taken were economics, natural history, senior forensics, mathematics, physics, geology, and chemistry.

By 1886, the year Clifford graduated, most course selections were purely discretionary, and a student's choice was limited only by his schedule and by any prerequisite course requirements. This new emphasis and direction at Harvard College had a profound impact on Clifford. Being able to choose courses that interested him, and subjects from which he could benefit the most, seemed to intensify his thirst for knowledge.

Clifford chose to major in science, a subject that had always intrigued him. He enjoyed researching various topics and having to quantify results in objective ways. Although he was a visionary who loved taking risks, he was glad for his professor's insistence that he learn to study scientific information carefully before giving opinions or making any rash decisions. It was an echo of his father's wise advice from a few years before. Making sure that he was basing his theories and reports on good, solid, "right" information would prove to be immensely valuable to him when he established his book companies.

Clifford's daily college routine began and ended with prayers, a practice which he relished and relied on despite the rigid regime.

Prayer had become important sustenance for his daily life. It wasn't until the first of the year in which Clifford graduated that President Eliot abolished compulsory chapel.[6] Although Clifford realized that doing so was an important component of the president's effort to provide students with choice, he was glad that Eliot had not instituted that change earlier. Chapel, daily prayer, and the teachings of the Bible had not only become an important part of Clifford's years at Harvard, they were also to become the bedrock of his life and business decisions.

Clifford lived on campus with a roommate, Alfred H. Lloyd, who became his lifelong friend and the man after whom Clifford was thought to have named his firstborn son. They shared a small, very pristine room in Massachusetts Hall which they promptly decorated in college dorm style.

Lloyd was a talented song writer who distinguished himself by writing the popular 1886 baccalaureate hymn "Time and Trust," a class song that remained one of the school's favorites. Clifford no doubt sang the tune as it was being written, and he probably played it often on the school's piano.

As he was on a very tight budget, most of Clifford's meals were taken on campus at the College Commons although he didn't particularly care for the food there. He was well aware that a student "could enjoy a fifty-cent table d'hotel dinners at one of the more popular eating places like Marliaves or have a beer and rabbit at Charlie Wirth's in town, and return to campus on the Owl Car from Bowdoin Square."[7] Joining his friends for trips into Cambridge for dinner was tempting, but Clifford's meager funds severely limited his participation.

Clifford's classmates also encouraged him to join them on trips to Boston to share in wild evenings with local chorus girls. But Clifford regularly declined. He had no real interest in anything he thought was morally or socially questionable. Other than a few dinners out and a few dates, he chose to spend his free time taking part in activities that were more wholesome and encouraged class solidarity, such as sitting with friends in the organized cheering sections at intercollegiate athletic events.

Clifford neither drank nor smoked at college (or afterward), and he eventually became an active member of the Harvard Total Abstinence League.[8] That organization is thought to have been associated with the Massachusetts Total Abstinence League that was active at the time.

The Harvard Total Abstinence League provided Clifford with the gentle and compassionate camaraderie he enjoyed most, as well as an opportunity to debate many of the most pressing issues of the day. His membership card, though tattered and dog-eared from use, would remain one of Clifford's most prized personal possessions, evoking happy collegiate memories that he often shared with his children.

Clifford's conservative ways were often judged to be excessively prudish by some of his more liberal-minded, free-spirited college friends, but that didn't seem to affect their respect or affection for him. Nor did it affect his self-confidence or his steadfast commitment to doing what he thought was morally right. Clifford was aggressively courted by many campus organizations that were searching for new members. His favorite group was the very popular Everett Athenaeum, a debating, drama, and music club that met every Friday night. He was officially elected to membership on October 19, 1883, during his sophomore year.[9]

As one of the group's more active members, Clifford soon became recognized for his effective debating skills. More often than not, he would purposely take the negative side of a debate (which he frequently lost) just to have the chance to articulate a less obvious and less popular view. Through his adoption of this unusual technique, he became highly skilled in research and debate procedures. His new skills would later provide the basis for a very successful college textbook series on debating that his publishing company would offer.

Clifford was quickly recognized as a polished public speaker, someone who was quite adept at expressing his position. He was also known as a very passionate debater. After losing a debate, he would often continue the discussion, amicably challenging his opponents for as many hours as they were willing to listen.

At a debate that took place on March 14, 1884, Clifford spoke for the negative on the question—"Resolved: That it is beneficial to students to work for honors." The affirmatives won on the merits of the argument—8 to 1.[10] But Clifford's position in this debate was certainly predictable because he was a strong believer in the importance of working for self-satisfaction and intellectual improvement rather than for honors. He believed that when honors became the goal, a student would likely not ever experience the sheer joy of learning for its own sake.

Clifford also distinguished himself as a polished impromptu speaker at Athenaeum meetings where he used his keen sense of humor and childhood experiences to regale his audience. He is reported to have made a five-minute impromptu speech on the topic "Things are Great," a speech that club members hailed as among his best. Indeed, things at Harvard *were* truly great for Clifford in those days, so there's little doubt that he simply spoke from the heart.

In addition to participating in speeches and debates, Clifford sang in the chorus in the school's musical productions, his melodious tenor voice clearly audible above the others. An instrumental musician, Clifford played both the banjo and the piano. His musical experiences in college reinforced his lifelong love of music and led him to later publish two very popular songbooks, *The Most Popular Home Songs* and *The Most Popular Hymns*. Clifford compiled both books while in college. These books include America's favorite songs and hymns from the turn of the century and can still be found in the Harvard Music Library today.[11]

Commencement

Clifford's senior year arrived with a stunning swiftness. His years at Harvard had gone by all too fast. Before he was ready to leave his intellectual sanctuary, it was time for the Class of 1886 to graduate.

The 1886 Harvard College graduating class numbered 223 of the brightest young minds of the day. Clifford received a Bachelor of Arts degree *cum laude*, with a major in science. His proud parents and his brothers and sister all attended the graduation exercises.

Graduation from Harvard was made especially memorable for Clifford because the ceremonies were steeped in tradition. From the first commencement in 1642 until the present day, there has been little or no change in the ceremony. Clifford had attended the graduation exercises during his earlier Harvard years, but there was nothing like the excitement of knowing that this one was his.

In her book, *Boston*, Nancy Sirkis describes the ceremony:

> Someone once said that the Harvard Commencement is the only true remaining American ritual. Far from being merely a magnificently staged graduation exercise, it is both a convention and a class day, and embodies much that both Harvard and Yankee Boston have traditionally stood for....
>
> The ceremonies begin with the arrival of the Governor of Massachusetts in a horse-drawn carriage...A procession is formed, led by the Sheriff of Middlesex County, suitably costumed for the occasion, followed by the President of the University, the top hatted Board of Overseers, and other dignitaries. The assembly is called to order by the sheriffs' striking the dais with the butt of his pikestaff. The graduating class then march to their seats, tipping their caps, as a voice admonishes them to do, to the statue of John Harvard.[12]

Clifford would later tell his amused family that very little was ever known about John Harvard. The statue created by Daniel Chester French was considered to be a purely imaginary portrait.

Clifford was mesmerized by the pomp and pageantry of his graduation exercises. He was determined to absorb and remember every detail of this watershed event in his young life. He listened intently to the graduate orations in Latin and English, occasionally glancing at the dignified President Eliot who occupied the ancient Tudor chair. *Mother and Father look so proud,* he thought, looking at his family, who also appeared to be totally engrossed in the ceremony.

Clifford was well aware of the fact that tuition, books, and clothing for his four years at Harvard had presented his parents with a significant hardship. They had also been shorthanded on the farm without him there. But Clifford had often voiced his appreciation, and he was confident that they were well pleased with their new Harvard graduate.

John McKinstry Merriam gave the Class Day Oration, and Alanson Bigelow Houghton delivered the Class Poem. After the orations, prayers, hymns, and an address in English, President Eliot presented the degrees to the graduates.[13] Then Eliot presented degrees to the graduates who were being awarded special honors. Clifford would never forget that walk across the lawn to receive his precious honors document. He was overwhelmed by the realization that he had not only become a Harvard graduate but that he had graduated with distinction. As he accepted his diploma and shook Eliot's hand, he was awestruck to hear the smiling president say, "Good work, Mr. Noble. You certainly did well. You kept your promise and you *have* made us proud. Congratulations."

As the benediction was delivered, Clifford silently offered his own words of thanks. Then the new graduates sang their class song. Clifford loved that song, and his parents could easily detect his loud, sweet tenor among his classmates' voices.

> *We sing a song of happy days,*
> *With hearts attuned to warmest praise.*
> *Together standing as of old, amid the elm trees green and gold.*
> *O here in final jubilee, our joy shall rouse these somber halls,*
> *In answer to our parting calls.*

The Commencement Day luncheon followed the ceremony. Lunch, consisting of freshly made chicken and potato salad, cold beer, and lemonade, was followed by another highlight—the colorful and traditional afternoon parade of Harvard alumni marching through Harvard Yard.[14] Clifford reveled in the thought that he would no doubt be joining them in the future. The alumni march was an event Clifford would long honor and enjoy.

The school's oldest living graduate led the parade, followed by aging graduates from decades gone by. Each alumnus wore a very legible nametag that displayed his name and year of graduation, and one member of each class carried a banner emblazoned with the appropriate year.

Howard, who sat pensively with Clifford and his family, watched the parade and beamed. But he had such conflicted feelings! He was proud of his older brother's accomplishments, but he also felt a sense of deep sadness that Clifford would be starting a whole new life without him.

Truth be known, Clifford himself was far from certain about the details of his immediate future. Unlike today, when most college graduates have a rather good idea of what they want to do with their lives, Clifford had not yet made a decision. In fact, most of his fellow students had not decided on careers by graduation day. Though he realized that careers in the church, medicine, and law were among the most popular vocations for new graduates, none of those interested him. But he *was* very sure about his decision to leave Cambridge and his home in rural Massachusetts to move to New York City.

Clifford wanted to be somebody in the corporate world; someone who would make a difference. He was well aware that New York had become the center of American book publishing, and several Harvard faculty members had encouraged him to consider that field. They understood his love of books, and he promised them that he would likely follow their advice.

Beyond Harvard

Immediately following graduation, Clifford returned to Westfield for a short visit and found that during his years at Harvard College, he had outgrown his hometown and neighbors.

At that time, the Westfield community was sorely lacking in any real social or business opportunities and Clifford was convinced that life there, at least for him, would be too mundane and uninteresting. The town lacked the intellectual stimulation and challenges that he had grown to depend upon at Harvard. Even his own brothers and sister had changed, and although he had not outgrown his close personal relationships with them, their lifestyles were far different from his.

After visiting with friends and former teachers and bidding a fond and tearful good-bye to his family, Clifford left for New York City. Howard had graduated from the Boston School of Mechanical Arts the same year, but he had decided to make his permanent home in Westfield. He later purchased the historic octagon house at #98 Court Street. Arthur had abandoned farm work for the business world, investing in a small local business of his own, and Julia was still at home.

Clifford was well aware that he was leaving behind all the people who were dearest to him, and that troubled him a bit. Rural Westfield was the only real home he'd ever known, and he was moving to a thriving urban metropolis. Although he had very limited funds and faced an unpredictable future, Clifford Noble was ready to go.

To help ease his transition from rural Westfield to urban New York, and to perfect the business skills he knew he would need to land a good job, he spent his summer attending the prestigious Eastman National Business College in Poughkeepsie, New York. The experience strengthened his self-confidence and job-finding savvy, and he felt well prepared for whatever lay ahead.

In the fall of 1886, the euphoric twenty-two-year-old Clifford Noble began his new life in New York City by walking the streets in search of a job. He was on his own, with no family in town, no contacts, and not one appointment. These obstacles might have discouraged other young men, but they were challenges to Clifford, ones that fueled his stubborn resolve to capitalize on his wonderful new opportunity to become successful and make a difference in the corporate world.

7

New York City

Clifford Noble, New York City, 1887

There are roughly three New Yorks.
There is, first, the New York of the man or woman who was born here, who takes the city for granted and accepts its size and its turbulence as natural and inevitable.
Second, there is the New York of the commuter—the city that is devoured by locusts each day and spat out each night.
Third, there is the New York of the person who was born somewhere else and came to New York in quest of something.
Of these three trembling cities the greatest is the last—the city of final destination, the city that is a goal.

—E. B. White, *New York*

◆   ◆   ◆

In our age of television, space travel, the computer, the cell phone, and the Internet, when innovation is often taken for granted, and the receipt of information about newsworthy events is instantaneous, we can only imagine the surprise, excitement, curiosity, and considerable apprehension Clifford must have felt during his first few days in New York City. He could not have been totally prepared for the New York scene. He made his way in those early years with very limited resources, and even faced some seemingly insurmountable challenges, but he never gave up or got sidetracked from what he wanted to accomplish, and he finally succeeded in making a difference.

Dark clouds had enveloped the city during the wee hours of the morning, and heavy rains and strong winds had been expected. But the sun finally managed to emerge triumphantly, allowing Clifford to later describe his first day in New York City as "a balmy, beautiful, sunny fall day."

G. Clifford Noble stood resolutely on a corner of upper Fifth Avenue that morning planning his job search, totally overwhelmed by his surroundings. Stephen Birmingham's *Life at the Dakota* describes a new visitor to New York, much like Clifford, as one who would be experiencing New York "as an astonishingly dirty city."

By 1885, some 250,000 horses pulling carts, carriages, trolleys and the six-horse team public omni-buses jammed New York's streets. The clatter of the horse-drawn traffic up and down Broadway continued day and night. Venturing out into the streets on foot was for the daring, and strollers encountered an obstacle course between piles of steaming dung which swarmed with flies...[1]

Despite his amazement of New York's condition, not quite what he had expected, the tolerant and exuberant Clifford must have felt uncomfortably provincial. He had never been in a city larger than Cambridge before. His thoughts and impressions, rather than being organized and specific, more than likely resembled a kaleidoscope of constantly changing colors, sounds, and smells of the city—all strong stuff for a New England country boy, Harvard graduate or not.

Upper Fifth Avenue was one of the ritziest neighborhoods in New York. Clifford marveled at the countless fancy stores and elaborate mansions that stood along this street and on those that surrounded nearby St. Patrick's Cathedral. It was hard for him to believe that this area, which now included beautiful Central Park, had once been a wasteland of wooden shacks, slums, and garbage dumps. New York City had acquired the 843-acre property in 1853, and over a long period of time had converted it into a magnificent system of heavily landscaped walkways, roads, and bridle paths.[2]

There was a very sophisticated retail shopping center up and down the avenue and on the streets nearby, with shops displaying such famous names as Macy's, Brooks Brothers, Black Starr & Frost, Tiffany's, Bonwit Teller & Company, Lord & Taylor's, Russeks, W & J Sloane, and Saks Fifth Avenue, all names that are still well-known today.

For Clifford, simply being in this vast metropolis, a place unlike any he had ever been, seemed surreal. Clifford was filled with both a sense of elation and joy, as well as a kind of strange anxiety that he had never known before as he considered the city's noise, dirt, and crowds. His observations must have been quite similar to those described by Judy Crichton in *America 1900*:

> Nothing in the city ever seemed complete, streets were torn up, buildings torn down, the city was in a state of perpetual regeneration. The traffic jams in the financial district rivaled those anywhere in the world. And the noise-the clanging trolleys, the steel-clad hooves on cobble streets, the hammering of the ironworkers on new construction, the babble of voices in a dozen different tongues, the nervous arrogant bell of the ambulance-all melded into one great city sound wave, tearing at the nerves of some, exhilarating others."[3]

It is difficult to fathom what Clifford's initial thoughts about New York really were. But from what he told his family members later, New York City—even those things that must have been annoying to others—seemed alive and promising to him. This was what he had dreamed of, and the reasons why he had decided to go to New York in the first place. New York, a soul-stirring urban complex, was his city of final destination: *his goal.*

He reveled in the realization, that despite what New York appeared to be, with all of its shortcomings, he had finally become a bona fide New Yorker—by attitude and choice, if not by birth. And he knew then, without a doubt, despite any apprehension or reservations he might have had earlier, that he was ready for this challenge.

Having grown up on the farm, where the daily work attire was overalls, a cotton shirt, and shoddy leather work shoes, Clifford was amazed by the sight of the affluent businessmen walking around in their fashionable English tweed jackets, flannel trousers, high shirt collars with flowing foulard neckties, and striking black top hats or fedoras. Many even carried handsome, carved wooden walking sticks. As he observed them with a keen and fascinated eye, he wondered what kind of job or social life each one had.

The women were even more elegant and bore no resemblance whatsoever to the simply dressed farmers' wives he'd known as a child. These women were impeccably coifed and attired, most dressed fashionably in long-skirted, colorful shirtwaists and long-sleeved blouses. Many of the women wore large-brimmed hats or torques—some with heavy veils, or carried dainty parasols to protect their flawless complexions from the sun and dust from the streets. Clifford couldn't help but admire their beauty, but he was saddened by the thought that his beloved mother had never had the chance to visit New York. He wondered how city life might have changed her. *Despite her active political life and hard work on the farm,* he thought, *it would have been wonderful for her to have the same opportunities as these women…and the same fabulous clothes.*

It became abundantly clear to Clifford that the New York City of the late 1880s was rapidly becoming the largest and most important city in America. This great city, with its one and a half million residents, a population twice what it had been only ten years earlier, was far larger than Clifford had thought possible when he was at Harvard. He realized that making a difference in a teeming city of this magnitude would likely be his life's biggest challenge.

Finding a Job

After moving into a small uptown hotel, Clifford began his job search, but he experienced several disappointing interviews during his first few days in the Upper Manhattan area. His meager funds were running frightfully low, but he needed to find an affordable, permanent home so he could concentrate on his job search.

After spending countless hours knocking on apartment house doors that displayed "For Rent" signs, Clifford finally found what he was looking for—a one-room efficiency apartment several blocks from lower Fifth Avenue. With his living accommodations settled, he began to rethink where in the city he might have the best chance of finding a job.

Equipped with a new game plan, Clifford walked the streets of Lower Manhattan; an area that seemed to cater to small businesses. He was still unclear about the kind of business he wanted to pursue, but he was alert to any new opportunities that might come his way. In a surprisingly short time, he happened upon what he initially believed to be a small retail bookstore. The establishment was managed by a friendly and seemingly successful individual by the name of Arthur Hinds.

Hinds was a longtime wholesale and retail book dealer in used public school and college books. He advertised his business as having "school books of all publishers at one store." He bought the books directly from distributors and from students searching for a place to sell their used books. Arthur Hinds & Company was located at Numbers 4, 5, 6, 12, 13, and 14 Cooper Institute in Manhattan—hardly the small store that Clifford originally visualized.

It is not clear whether Clifford had finally focused his job search on the bookselling industry when he applied for a job with Arthur Hinds, but we do know that bookselling was a subject that definitely interested him. Manhattan dominated the post–Civil War publishing scene in America at the time. Many of the major publishing houses were located there and all of the major booksellers had established one or more Manhattan stores.

1886, the year Clifford arrived in New York City, was a historic one. Annette Witheridge best describes it in *New York—Then and Now* as a date that marked the unveiling of France's spectacular gift to America, the magnificent Statue of Liberty. "The statue is known the world over as the symbol of America and provided the first glimpse of New York for millions of immigrants arriving by boat....Designed by Frederic Auguste Bartholdi, the 225-ton, 151-foot-tall statue is based on a likeness of his mother."[4]

1886 also marked the year in which Clifford Noble entered the employ of Arthur Hinds as a book salesman and clerk. In a strange way Clifford found amazing similarities between these two events. By coming to New York, both he and the immigrants were being afforded an opportunity for an exciting new beginning.

Although Clifford had no direct sales experience other than that he had gained as a young boy, he *was* a Harvard graduate, and Mr. Hinds was quite aware of his many other appealing assets, including his obvious passion for books. But Hinds' deciding factor for hiring Clifford was that he was not married. Hinds believed that Clifford would make an excellent employee simply because he wouldn't have any outside distractions and could therefore be totally devoted to his duties at the store. Hinds invited Clifford to join his company as a clerk, and Clifford enthusiastically accepted.

Clifford began his new job in the fall of 1886, and he was almost immediately euphoric about his work. He tackled even the most tedious housekeeping chores, such as dusting and organizing the hundreds of shelved books in the store, sweeping the floors, and monitoring the store's inventory, with a unique dedication and contagious enthusiasm.

Hinds took note and appreciated having Clifford on hand for such routine chores; having a good employee gave the owner more time to concentrate on the details of running the business. As he watched Clifford handle his day's assignment on his first day in the store, Hinds could see that the young man had the makings of a proper bookseller.

Clifford Noble was hired for a weekly salary of $8.33. He committed to receiving that amount for a period of three years. This was a paltry sum, even in those days, and it meant that he had to restrict himself to an extremely tight budget.

Farm life had spoiled Clifford for hearty, home-cooked meals. He had looked forward to eating in the excellent New York restaurants that he'd heard so much about, especially after having endured the often tasteless meals he was served in Harvard's dining commons. But it didn't take him long to realize that he couldn't afford to eat out and pay rent on his meager paycheck. So lunch was usually limited to a corned beef sandwich and a mug of sarsaparilla. He could buy both for a nickel at a nearby café. Once in a while he would splurge on a lunch at one of his favorite, lavishly appointed Shrafft's restaurants. There he would indulge himself with gourmet chicken salad or a freshly roasted turkey sandwich served with fresh fruit or hard-boiled eggs. These meals were expensive, however, and were a treat Clifford only rarely permitted himself.

Never one to become easily discouraged, Clifford came up with an idea that he felt would not only save him some money, but would also increase business at the store. He knew that he'd have to convince Mr. Hinds, however, so he scheduled an appointment with his employer one afternoon when there were few shoppers around.

Living at the Store

"I have a special request of you, Mr. Hinds," Clifford began, wasting no time in broaching the subject, as Hinds, perched on a stepladder, busily arranged books on an upper shelf.

"I'd like to move into your store and sleep here rent free," Clifford said. "I really don't make enough money to do much else." His astonished employer stared at him as if he was quite sure that Clifford did not understand what he was asking, and then quickly stepped down from the ladder to face Clifford directly.

"That's out of the question," Hinds stated flatly after an uncomfortable pause. "Whatever made you come up with such a foolish idea?"

"I've given this a lot of thought," Clifford said, convinced, despite Mr. Hinds' obvious reluctance, that his plan was a good one. "Think about the advantages of allowing me to live here. There are at least two good reasons why you should agree."

Clifford continued, in his usual methodical style. "First, you'd be assured that someone would be on the premises at all times, so you'd be able to save the money you've been spending on store security.

"Second, I'd be in the store full-time, so we can be much more flexible with our store hours. I could work evenings and weekends. That schedule would attract many more customers for us, like the ones who work and are unable to shop during the day."

As Clifford continued to present his very persuasive arguments, using many of the debating techniques that he had developed at Harvard, Mr. Hinds sat back in his chair and listened. After a long and almost intolerable silence, he finally tossed his hands up in the air and exclaimed, "Okay, Clifford. I must admit you present a very convincing case. We'll try it. I do find the idea of extended store hours intriguing, although I'm not at all sure that you will like making the store your home."

"You won't regret it, sir," Clifford assured him as the two men stood and shook hands. "Thank you."

"You may be right, Clifford," Hinds replied, smiling for the first time since the meeting had begun. "At least, I certainly hope you are."

What the very conservative Mr. Hinds had unwittingly done that day, by permitting Clifford to introduce some creative new ways to conduct business, was establish a culture within the store that Clifford Noble would later replicate in his own businesses. It was a culture that would feed Clifford's entrepreneurial spirit and provide him with many unexpected opportunities. It was one that allowed him to take risks and try new things that would ultimately establish his reputation in the bookselling business as one of the city's top professionals.

Elated by the success of his proposal, Clifford moved out of his old apartment the very next day. Fortunately, his landlord was sympathetic to his financial plight and agreed to let him break his lease without penalty.

An appreciative Clifford gathered his few personal possessions together as quickly as possible. True, he'd have to carry his belongings by hand onto the crowded public omnibus and handle any further moving arrangements by himself, but the luxury of free rent made any inconvenience he might encounter worth the extra effort.

With the omnibus ride behind him, a daring Clifford carefully made his way across several city blocks to the store, dodging unruly horse-drawn carriages and side stepping piles of dung. Encumbered by his heavy satchel, he staggered through the storefront door and dropped his bag just inside the threshold. It was after hours, and the hushed quiet of the darkened bookstore seemed a bit foreboding. Clifford quickly locked the door behind him and carried his bag to a small back room that was full of boxes and stacks of books. He realized for the first time that his new living quarters were far from ideal and hardly something he could call home.

Clifford was accustomed to the small living quarters he'd shared with his roommate at Harvard, but the bookstore offered no kitchen or full bathroom. He would be forced to sleep on a hard and lumpy floor pallet, and he'd have to use the store's bathroom sink for bathing and laundering his clothes.

As Clifford began to unpack, he also quickly realized there were no closets or bureaus. But determined to make the best of things, he laid his few clothes out on the floor in one inconspicuous corner and told himself that the arrangement would just have to work. Eventually he would improvise a table and chairs from the numerous wooden and cardboard shipping boxes that arrived at the store almost daily.

Clifford soon learned to store bottled, boxed, and bagged food supplies in the small cupboard beneath the bathroom sink. This action helped him cut down on having to eat out so often. Fortunately, his formative years on the farm had taught him to live frugally and to appreciate the simpler things of life, so he was rarely tempted to take in New York's expensive nightlife.

All in all, Clifford was grateful for the free living arrangements, and he concluded that the situation did offer some relatively attractive advantages. When he finally lay down to sleep that first night, satisfied that he'd done the right thing, Clifford was lulled by the intoxicating scent of the hundreds of leather-bound books that lined the bookstore's shelves. As he dozed off, he wondered what new possibilities the morrow would bring.

One benefit of his new living arrangements that Clifford could not have foreseen was the shelter the bookstore provided him during the historic blizzard of March 12, 1888. The storm totally shut down New York City for three days.

Public transportation was unavailable as no trains or trolleys were running. Carts and carriages were left abandoned on city streets and were buried by the snow. Schools, stores and businesses, and even the post office and public offices were indefinitely closed.

In his book, *Life at the Dakota,* Birmingham reported that "some 15,000 New Yorkers were trapped in elevated trains on tracks that had become blocked by snow drifts, and a number of enterprising souls made a tidy business out of raising ladders from the street and helping passengers climb down, at a dollar a head. At least one train that was too high for a ladder to reach was stalled in the air for sixteen hours while the passengers were kept from freezing with whiskey that was hoisted up from the street by ropes."[5] Tragically, several hundred people lost their lives in this storm.

The blizzard, with its high winds and blinding snow, gave Clifford a welcome reprieve from his daily assignment of dusting the shelves, sorting mail, taking inventory, distributing and cataloguing books, and keeping track of all sales and new book orders. Clifford kept warm by the bookstore's small coal stove, tried to make himself comfortable on the floor, ate whatever he could find in his makeshift pantry and, with an unlimited inventory of good books to choose from, read. He quickly became an expert on Hinds' inventory.

Building the Store's Business

Living at the store enabled Clifford to expand store hours and subsequently increase sales. In fact, he quickly earned himself quite a reputation as a knowledgeable, very accessible Manhattan book salesman. Customer satisfaction, as measured by an increase in repeat business, was at an all-time high.

The well-stocked Arthur Hinds & Company bookstore was staffed with a small but growing cadre of intelligent assistants. They all loved books, and the store increasingly mirrored the small, almost extinct family-owned bookstore of today, one in which the salespeople are all personally familiar with the books in their inventory. Clifford found no difficulty selling books because he offered his customers something he knew and loved. He provided his customers with enthusiastic, highly personalized service, thereby endearing himself to them. Much like Geoffrey Faber described books in *A Publisher Speaking,* Clifford believed that "books are the life-blood of a civilized society. Without books, science, history, philosophy, the drama, and the novel could not exist at all…. Without books there would be no accumulation of knowledge…or communication between the ages…"[6]

Clifford also believed that good books offered the readers interesting new subjects that they could discuss with their well read friends and business associates setting themselves above the mundane, common citizen. He tried to entice his customers into buying those books he thought they should read, and he was usually quite successful. Customers searching for interesting new titles sought him out for recommendations.

At Clifford's insistence, the bookstore was made quite homelike and inviting. By its very appearance, it encouraged prospective buyers and readers to drop in frequently and casually browse through the volumes on the shelves. Comfortable overstuffed chairs were carefully arranged to provide cozy spots for single customers or groups to congregate. As in the Barnes & Noble superstores of today, lingering, lounging customers were always welcome. Clifford was a strong advocate of the philosophy that *how* the store did business was just as important as *how much* business it did. That unique *modus operandi* contributed to the store's soaring profits, and Arthur Hinds & Company quickly became a very popular destination for book buyers on the New York scene.

In the decade from 1880 to 1890, the school textbook business was a fiercely competitive one. John Barnes Pratt wrote in his *Personal Recollections* that "it was an especially difficult time for that industry because the monopoly concept was sweeping the country." (U.S. Steel, Standard Oil, and U.S. Lines were formed in this period.)[7] It affected the textbook industry as well. In 1890, the two largest textbook companies merged as the American Book Company, acquiring the textbook operations of the next two largest firms. Eventually they acquired thirty other firms and for a short period of time, the American Book Company held 93 percent of the nation's textbook business.

The largest company to remain independent was Ginn & Company. Edwin Ginn, company president declined to join their syndicate in a letter describing the various reasons why he did not believe that a monopoly would work well in textbook industry. Hinds, for one, would certainly be at a disadvantage when it came to competitive pricing. Ginn was right. The American Book Company's market share began to fall until it amounted to barely 6 percent, and over the next several years a host of new companies, including Hinds & Noble, began to take its place.

By the late 1890s, Clifford had a wife and three children, and he had discovered that bookselling was not only fiercely competitive, but also far more challenging than he'd originally envisioned. He had learned that the bookseller must satisfy a number of different groups of customers in order to stay ahead of the competition.

Maintaining a broad inventory of books was essential, but most booksellers, like Arthur Hinds, had a limited amount of money to invest in stock. Accordingly, they had to stay current on what used book titles, and especially textbook titles, would likely be popular and in demand during the coming year. It was no longer feasible or profitable to merely stock, arrange, and dust books on the shelves while waiting for customers to walk through the door. The prosperous booksellers had to be adept at predicting what would sell the following year, stock those titles, and then build a customer base and market for those books.

When he started with Hinds, two of Clifford's primary assets were his recent graduation from a premier institution of higher learning and his continued close contacts with college faculty. His ability to identify with his young customers and gain "insider knowledge" about the texts likely to be required reading the following year made him an outstanding salesman and a valued and trusted advisor to his employer. In fact, his remarkable ability to identify what books the public schools would likely buy is analogous to Barnes & Noble's growing power today to determine what America reads.

Arthur Hinds did not hesitate to buy the titles Clifford recommended. They always sold quickly, allowing the business to grow and prosper. As their business and their reputation as knowledgeable booksellers grew, Clifford recognized still another new opportunity. He suggested to Hinds that they begin their own publishing company. The idea was enthusiastically accepted.

Many years later, "An Obituary Note" about Clifford that appeared in The Publishers Weekly—June 13, 1936, noted that "Arthur Hinds & Company was not only a jobber of books of all companies and able to supply any school book published at better prices than any other house in the country, but through its totally new and separate publishing house it began to publish books under its own imprint."

One of the company's most popular publications was an 88-volume series Handy Literal Translations, which included English translations of Latin and other classical works. At first schools frowned upon these "ponies" because they were viewed as a means for students to cheat on translation assignments. In time, however, the books were accepted as legitimate scholastic aids in the classical courses, Eventually they became highly recommended and were used by public and private schools and colleges throughout the nation.

The academic bookselling and book publishing business of Arthur Hinds continued to prosper. When Clifford began working for the company, it occupied four stores in the Cooper Union Building, which James D. McCabe Jr. describes in his book, New York By Gaslight:

Cooper Union occupied the triangular space formed by the junction of the Bowery, Third and Fourth Avenues and 7th Street. It was a plain but massive and imposing edifice of brownstone, six stories high, with a large basement below the level of the streets. It was erected by (prominent New Yorker) Peter Cooper in 1857, at a cost of $630,000, and was operated as one of the first schools in the country to provide a free education to the working class children and women. The street floor was let out to stores, and the floor above was occupied by offices of various kinds (such as those of Arthur Hinds). These floors and the great hall in the basement yielded a handsome revenue, which was devoted to paying a part of the expenses of the institution. The remainder of the building was devoted to a free library and reading room, and halls for lectures and for study.[8]

The Institute was an ideal location for Arthur Hind's bookstore because it offered Hinds good visibility and an excellent public image.

But Hinds' opportunity to lease space in the Institute was short-lived. An enormous endowment made to Cooper Union by steel magnate Andrew Carnegie, the richest man in the world at that time, made it unnecessary for Cooper Union to rent out building space any longer. Arthur Hinds and the smaller publishing companies located there, such as E & J B Young, Wilbur Ketcham, and Robert Trent Publishers were all forced to relocate. Hinds moved his business to 31-33-35 West 15th Street which adjoined the St. Francis Xavier School and College, a site the company would remain at for fifteen years.

8

A Chance Encounter in Central Park

Lizzie Adams and Clifford Noble, 1890

The meeting of two personalities is like the contact of two chemical substances; if there is any reaction, both are transformed.

—Carl Jung

◆   ◆   ◆

A love story may seem out of place among descriptions of the book business in the big city, but Clifford Noble was never one to overlook an opportunity. His chance encounter with Lizzie Adams and the courtship that ensued felt "right" to Clifford. As always, he followed his instincts, and this time they led to a lifelong relationship that helped to enrich and define his life.

One unusually busy day at the bookstore during the early 1890s, Clifford decided he needed to take some time off from work. For months he'd spent day and night at the store, with little or no respite from his duties. He'd made no time for any sort of life of his own and found himself feeling agitated and disagreeable despite the store's increasing sales. He hoped that perhaps his employer would agree to give him a little time away from the store, an action that would benefit them both.

Clifford finished tallying the bill for what appeared to be the last patron of the day, saw the customer to the door, and then made his move. "Excuse me, Mr. Hinds," he said. "May I please speak with you a moment, sir?" Clifford began helping his employer collate and add up the day's receipts.

"Of course, Clifford. What is it?" Hinds closed his cash register and turned to give Clifford his full attention.

"Well, sir, I was wondering whether I might take a few days off from work." Clifford had decided it would be best to get right to the point.

Mr. Hinds stood quietly for a moment and then smiled. "You'll not believe this, Clifford," he said, "but I've been wondering how long it would take you to realize that a little rest—not too much rest, mind you—is good for the soul. Of course you may, Clifford. Enjoy yourself with my blessing."

Clifford was somewhat incredulous. "Really? I wasn't prepared for you to say yes so quickly."

Hinds laughed. The young man's sincerity and candor appealed to him. "If anyone deserves a little vacation, my boy, it's you. You've been a real asset to the business, and you've earned some time off. Why not start tomorrow?"

"I'd like that," Clifford replied. "But are you sure you'll be able to manage alone?"

"I think I can do that," an amused Hinds said, remembering the many years he had been both owner and sole employee of his business.

The next day Clifford rose early, not wishing to miss a single moment of his two days off by sleeping late. He decided that he wanted to go horseback riding in Central Park. Riding was an enormously popular recreation in that day, and hundreds of public and private stables dotted the New York City area. But Clifford thought it would probably be easiest to hire a good mount at the Central

Park Riding Academy so he could enjoy a leisurely ride through the park. He had read a great deal about Central Park's history, and its breathtaking landscape, with its many miles of lush, well-manicured bridle trails. He was also aware that it was the favorite destination of thousands of New Yorkers, offering them all manner of recreational opportunities in addition to horseback riding; a thought that made his day off at the Park all the more exciting. Clifford was delighted with his chance to spend some time there.

Confident he wouldn't be seeing anyone he knew, he dressed quickly in his faded blue overalls, a wrinkled blue and white checked cotton shirt, and an old pair of scuffed riding boots that he'd worn on the family farm. There was still a bit of the country boy in him, and the old clothes seemed appropriate. They were also just plain comfortable.

Clifford was a nice-looking young man who had always been careful about his personal appearance, and he managed to look relatively fashionable even in his somewhat unkempt work clothes. He had neatly combed his thick head of light brown hair that morning before tucking it under his comfortable old cap, and he was clean-shaven, save for his distinctive moustache which he had grown following graduation—sort of a rite of passage from Harvard to the next stage of his life. Hard work and a frugal lifestyle had kept him lean and fit, and he made a rather dashing figure as he left the store to spend his first real day off from his often taxing job.

The sun was just beginning to peek over the easterly horizon as he left his apartment, sending out its first inviting rays of sunshine that foretold a perfect day. Clifford was filled with lofty expectations and curiosity about what the day would bring.

He took the streetcar to the stop nearest the riding academy (which survived until 1916) and walked the remaining distance. Once he reached the stable, he judiciously scanned the horses that were tied to the hitching post just outside the entrance, pleased that he had such a wide selection to choose from.

"See anything you like?" the seasoned stable hand asked. A jolly smile lit up the man's rugged face.

"That one there," Clifford said, pointing to a frisky oversized stallion at the far end of the line.

"Good choice," the stable hand replied. "Star's a beauty. He's a favorite among the many equestrians we accommodate here, to be sure."

No doubt, Clifford thought. The bay's sleek, reddish brown hide and jet black mane fairly shouted health and vitality. A brilliant splash of white on the magnificent horse's forehead had given Star not only his name but his regal look as well.

Exuberant, Clifford quickly mounted the horse. After positioning his boots securely in the stirrups, he gathered the reins and guided Star in a slow trot down the well-worn dirt bridle path. It had been some time since he'd ridden a horse, but old habits die slowly. It took him no time at all to feel confident about his riding ability and to comfortably gain the feel of the animal.

The well-trained and highly responsive horse seemed totally familiar with the path, so Clifford had little to do but sit back and let the horse have his head and allow his mount to take *him* for a ride. As the cool early morning breeze blew softly on his cheeks, Clifford verbally coaxed Star from a trot into a canter and then to a smooth, rhythmical gallop. He gently prodded the animal with the tip end of his boot. Star instinctively responded to his every movement. *This is wonderful*, Clifford told himself. *Why on earth did it take me so long to do this?*

After a while, Clifford slowed the horse and glanced at his watch. Although he'd been riding for more than an hour, he'd been totally unaware of the passage of time on the trail. *Funny*, he thought, *how unimportant time can sometimes be.* After all, his life at the bookstore seemed to be dictated solely by the clock.

Clifford had forgotten how much fun it was to ride a *good* horse! Old Tom and Kitty, his father's farm horses, were quite old and very slow. Riding them had often just been an exercise in patience. At one time his father had used the animals to pull the family buggy and help with some of the farm work, but he had really kept them around of late because Clifford and his siblings loved them dearly. Although he thought of them often, Clifford hadn't ridden either horse since he left for college and he couldn't help but wonder on this day what his father might do with them. He worried that his father might decide that maintaining the two nonproductive, aging horses was too costly an option. The thought made him sad, so he chose to concentrate on enjoying his special day off.

Clifford rode down the trail totally engrossed in the moment, oblivious to the other riders nearby. The colorful wildflowers and the bright yellow forsythia that were in full bloom all along the bridle path were magnificent! He was also intrigued by the many birds and small animals along the way. He watched nature's show with contented amusement—the sparrows and robins searching for seeds and insects, and the frisky, playful gray squirrels darting across his path. They all reminded him of springtime in Westfield and his happy boyhood days at the "zoo."

Clifford had certainly picked the ideal time of the year to experience his first horseback ride in New York. *It's the perfect spring day,* he told himself, *just as springtime in New York is known to be.* He loosened up on the reins and prepared to continue his relaxed, stress-free ride.

Rider in Distress

All of a sudden, without any warning, Clifford was jolted out of his peaceful ride by the frantic cries of a rider several yards ahead.

"Help!" the rider called. "Will someone please help me?" The anxious plea came several more times, increasing in intensity each time.

Clifford quickly reined in Star and assessed the situation. A panicked female rider, clinging desperately to the mane of her runaway horse, was struggling to keep from falling off and possibly being trampled to death. The cinch had come loose, causing the sidesaddle to dip dangerously downward toward the bridle path. The farther the saddle slid, the more desperate were the woman's cries for help. Clifford could see that the woman's long, sapphire colored skirt had become entangled beneath her, and having lost her reins, she was rapidly losing control of her beautiful chestnut mare.

As Clifford was the closest rider to her, he did not hesitate to react. He coaxed Star into a rapid gallop and within minutes, he reached the terrified rider's side.

Leaning over his saddle, he reached for her dangling reins. Just when he had given up hope of trying to secure them, the mare faltered slightly, giving Clifford the advantage that he'd been hoping for.

"Whoa, my pretty girl," he shouted, tightening her reins and eventually slowing down her horse. In a matter of minutes, he had brought both mounts to a total standstill. "Steady now, steady", he said, in a voice just above a whisper as the agitated mare stomped and snorted, eventually calming to Clifford's soothing voice.

Then Clifford dismounted. Maintaining a tight grip on the mare's reins with one hand, he assisted the woman with the other as she slid down from her horse. Then he tightened the mare's wayward cinch.

When the female rider turned to thank him, Clifford was surprised to discover that she appeared to be in her twenties, most likely his own age, and quite comely.

"Thank you so much!" she said in a breathless voice. "Talk about timing. I don't know what I would have done if you hadn't come along."

"Are you all right?" Clifford asked.

"Just shaken up a bit," she replied, brushing off her skirt and trying to compose herself. "And embarrassed. I'm usually a rather good rider," she added with a touch of modest pride. "I've never ridden this particular mare before, but I've also never has trouble with any of the other Academy horses."

"Most likely something spooked her," Clifford reasoned.

"You're probably right. I do remember a couple of street urchins sitting on the overpass a short way back. They were tossing pebbles at the horses passing by. I tried to avoid them. But it looks as though one of those pebbles may have hit my horse's rump." She gave a little shrug and continued, "Well, whatever it was, I'm just grateful that you were in the park today. Thank you."

This girl intrigued Clifford, and as he studied her for a brief moment, he concluded that she was a wholesome looking brunette of medium build, with strong facial features and piercing blue eyes. She wasn't exceptionally beautiful in the traditional sense, but her genteel appearance and her friendly way totally disarmed him.

"No thanks are necessary," he told her politely. "I'm just glad that I could be of assistance."

"I'm Elizabeth Adams," she volunteered. "But my friends and family call me Lizzie. You can too, if you wish," she added.

"And I'm Clifford Noble, Lizzie," he replied. "May I walk you back to the stables, or do you think you'll be able to ride back?"

"Thank you, Clifford, for being so thoughtful, but I think I can ride," she responded. And then, as if scolding herself for being a little afraid, she quickly added, "Of course I can ride. I'll be just fine,"

Clifford chuckled to himself, amused by her spunk, independence, and determination. She didn't appear to be at all phased by her terrifying experience and he liked that about her.

He had not previously been interested in any particular girl. Even at Harvard, although he had a few dates with girls from Cambridge, he had never really been interested in pursuing any of those relationships. Perhaps he had been too busy or too involved in academic pursuits, or maybe he had simply never found anyone remarkable enough to capture his interest. Whatever the case, he found himself totally smitten by Lizzie.

On their ride back to the Academy and horse stables, the two equestrians kept their conversation light. Lizzie told Clifford a bit about her family and her recent graduation from Vassar College. Clifford was delighted to discover that they shared the same graduation year from two of the nation's outstanding colleges. They talked about their love of New York City and they seemed to have a great deal in common. By the time they reached the Academy, Clifford knew that he definitely wanted to pursue a friendship with Lizzie.

Lizzie's official Vassar College graduation photo—1886.

"Thank you again, Clifford," she said as they dismounted and handed their horses over to the stable hand.

"You're very welcome. I'm certainly glad this experience is over with and I hope you will allow me to see you home," Clifford said.

Lizzie thanked him but told him that her father would be coming to pick her up. So Clifford offered to stay with her until her father arrived.

Then Lizzie totally surprised him when she coyly added, "I'd love to have you visit me sometime, Clifford. I live at 32 East 63rd Street, which really isn't very far from here."

This young woman must be reading my mind, Clifford thought, pleased beyond words that she had extended an invitation to continue their relationship. "That would be my pleasure, Lizzie," he said, careful not to sound overly interested.

Clifford and Lizzie chatted a bit about the beautiful day and some of the nearby New York attractions. But all too soon, a distinguished-looking, middle-aged man with a heavy dark beard arrived in one of those rarely seen, fancy new chauffeur-driven automobiles. Since Lizzie had given Clifford her 63rd Street address—in one of the more affluent sections of the city—Clifford had no trouble figuring out who the man's passenger would be. As the car pulled up in front of the stables, a gentleman, quite obviously Lizzie's father, emerged from the back seat to warmly greet Lizzie. Then they both got into the automobile and promptly drove off with their chauffer at the steering wheel.

Too intimidated to wait for an introduction, Clifford had bid Lizzie a hasty farewell from afar. He waved good-bye to her as she watched him from the rear window. She returned the gesture along with a warm smile, and Clifford was surprised by the sweet rush of joy and longing that shimmered through his body. He had never felt this way about anyone else before. *Yes*, he told himself, *I have no doubt that I shall be seeing Lizzie Adams again.*

A Flourishing Romance

Early the next day, Clifford sent a large, impressive bouquet of fresh spring flowers to Lizzie's fashionable brownstone home on East 63rd Street. The spray included beautiful yellow daffodils, white daisies with brilliant yellow sunburst centers, and a complement of airy baby's breath. He'd inserted a handwritten card that read: "Thinking about you, and hope you are doing well."

The bouquet represented the first purchase of its kind that Clifford had ever made and one that he could ill afford. He'd also never written a personal note to a girl before, so he was unsure about the appropriateness of either one, but he wanted Lizzie to know how he felt.

As it turned out, Lizzie was delighted with his thoughtfulness and concern. She admired the bouquet as though it had been arranged by Clifford himself, and the fresh spring scent of the flowers seemed to fill the room. She had been quite taken by Clifford herself, but she was surprised by Clifford's interest. They seemed to really like one another which made her very happy, and their lifetime relationship began that very day.

Clifford and Lizzie loved being together from the start. They shared many weeks thereafter getting acquainted with each other and acquainted with New York City. They spent some of their free time shopping at Macy's and other fancy Manhattan shops, listening to soapbox orators at Union Square, attending public parties in Central Park, enjoying various cultural events, and even taking in a New York baseball game. Their favorite place however, perhaps for sentimental reasons, was Central Park. Apart from frequent horseback rides in the park, they often went there for picnics. They loved to watch the small schoolboys, dressed in their stylish middy blouses with sailor collars and navy pants, sitting on the grass, sailing their miniature yachts on Lily Pond.

As Lizzie stood nearby, one of the young sailors would always invite Clifford to join them to try his hand at launching one of their little boats. Clifford would eagerly accept their invitation and settle himself beside the boys on the grass. He loved being with them and they seemed to enjoy being with him. Despite their age difference, they laughed a lot together as they staged their sailing races. With Clifford's help and counsel, each boy happily learned to position his boat in such a way that would allow him to take advantage of the breezes and increase his boat's speed. The boys took great delight when they won a race—especially when they beat Clifford. Competition was keen. And when it was finally time to leave, Clifford and Lizzie, and the boys, reluctantly said good-bye.

In the winter, when the ball was up at Central Park, they would go ice skating. According to Birmingham in *Life at the Dakota*, "In winter, the lake and the pond at Fifty-Ninth street quickly made skating the most important pastime for rich and poor alike. When the public horse carts and omnibuses sported colored flags, it meant that 'the ball is up in the Park'—a balloon that was raised to let people know that the ice was safe for skating. Tens of thousands of New Yorkers would subsequently flock to Central Park to waltz and figure skate on the park's frozen waters. At night the ice was lighted with many calcium lamps to illuminate the Currier and Ives scene."[1]

Early in the skating season, at Lizzie's insistence, Clifford reluctantly agreed to exchange his farm clothes for the popular male skating attire—a derby hat, overcoat, and long pants, all of which he had bought for the occasion with his limited funds, so he looked quite appropriate, and Lizzie, of course, could always be counted on to be dressed in the latest, fashionable long skirted skating outfit.

At the park, a young male attendant was generally available to help Lizzie put on her skates. On those perfect crisp and clear winter evenings after Lizzie and Clifford finished skating, their cheeks and noses ruddy from the biting winter cold, the park employee would help Lizzie remove her skates and don her stylish fur-lined snow boots. Then he served the two shivering skaters steaming cups of delectable hot chocolate. Those were memorable evenings for both of them, and ones that they would talk about for years thereafter.

On one such occasion, a few weeks after the two had met, Lizzie looked especially stunning in her newly purchased long ruby red dress and white fur-trimmed coat, matching earflaps, and fur muff. Clifford was quick to take notice and was lavish with his compliments. "You're lovely, Lizzie," he said, as she openly blushed. "I'm quite sure that you must know by now that I'm becoming more attracted to you each day." And Clifford cautiously reached out to hold Lizzie's hand.

"It's a funny thing, Clifford," Lizzie responded, lovingly stroking his hand. "We have had such fun together. I'll never forget the day we met while horseback riding at the park. What started out to be a very bad day, ended up being a wonderful one.

"But it's like you always say, Clifford, when your heart is really open to God's enduring love, miracles do happen. Who would have thought that *we* would meet in Central Park with me on a *runaway* horse? It was hardly the romantic meeting that I had dreamed about or what I had imagined divine intervention to be. I think that He must have planned our first encounter in a moment of distraction."

Clifford nodded his head in agreement and laughed heartily.

9

From Holidays to Partnerships

I will honor Christmas in my heart and try to keep it all the year.

—Charles Dickens

◆   ◆   ◆

For Clifford Noble, the 1890s brought courtship, bereavement, and matrimony, and ended with a decision that would have a wonderful and lasting benefit for Clifford and his family. Throughout the decade, Clifford showed his deep affinity for the holiday season and the opportunities they provided for wonderful, memorable family gatherings.

Christmas in New York City in 1891, even with the usual harsh weather and snow-packed streets, resembled a magical winter wonderland. Thousands of tapered icicles hung from the branches of the trees, and the newly fallen snow covering the streets and walkways glistened in the bright sun.

Even Mr. Hinds had joined in the spirit of the season by decorating the bookstore in his usual modest style. He had placed a three-foot-tall live spruce tree on the checkout counter and adorned it with a few colorful Christmas balls. Beside it he placed a simple wooden Nativity scene. In his store windows, he had hung a couple of small, freshly cut aromatic Christmas wreaths decorated with red velvet bows.

Clifford appreciated his employer's effort to celebrate the season because he knew that Christmas held a special meaning for the devout Mr. Hinds. Unlike Mr. Scrooge in Charles Dickens's book, *A Christmas Carol*, the frugal Mr. Hinds cherished Christmas as a season of generosity and great joy. He was deeply disturbed that in their secular society, Christmas had become so commercialized. But despite his distaste for the extravagant spending by many Christmas shoppers, Mr. Hinds was more than generous himself when it came to extending warm Christmas greetings to his customers and providing much appreciated small holiday bonuses to Clifford and his other employees.

Still, Mr. Hinds's ever-so-prudent and thrifty adornments were totally overshadowed by the many extravagant Christmas displays on show throughout the city. These displays enticed busy shoppers already laden with colorfully wrapped packages to shop some more. But Clifford and Lizzie seemed oblivious to the temptation to spend. On their many walks throughout the city, they simply enjoyed the decorations, letting the Christmas spirit warm their souls.

As the young couple meandered down Fifth Avenue, a small group of Christmas carolers would occasionally appear from out of nowhere, position themselves at a store's entrance or on the steps of a church, and sing the season's familiar songs. This was one of Clifford's favorite holiday traditions. He rarely resisted the opportunity to chime in or at least hum along—often in harmony with the makeshift street choir.

At times, a robust-looking white-bearded fellow dressed in a Santa Claus outfit would dash by, obviously trying to make his way to some store in which he was scheduled to hold court. The Santa would politely fend off the excited children who dogged him along the way.

Although Clifford had a very limited amount of disposable money to spend, that never seemed to matter to him or to Lizzie. Both were more than content to simply hold hands, trek through the mantle of snow that blanketed the city streets, and window-shop. Bundled up in warm coats, scarves, and mittens to insulate themselves from the biting air, they walked down Fifth Avenue admiring the seductive store-window displays and acknowledging the many passersby who offered warm Christmas greetings.

The Christmas spirit was contagious, and Lizzie often wished aloud that the spirit of the season could be sustained throughout the year. "Christmas gives us the chance to show the power of God's love to one another," she said to Clifford. "What a peaceful and beautiful world it would be if we could all be inspired to share more of His love with each other, every day of the year, wherever we go, and whatever we do."

Lizzie and Clifford were both mesmerized by the FAO Schwartz toy store windows, crowds of onlookers stopped to gaze at the mechanized toys and the delightful miniature train that blew smoke and chugged its way through a small town decorated for Christmas. Lizzie and Clifford laughed when they saw the lovely talking dolls that had attracted some wide-eyed little girls dressed up in their Sunday finest. The girls peered at the displays and happily chattered with one another about their favorite doll. Their well-dressed parents quickly joined them and they all disappeared into the store, only to emerge a short time later with Christmas boxes that Lizzie identified as "doll boxes."

Clifford and Lizzie walked a few blocks toward other parts of the fascinating city. In *America 1900*, Judy Crichton describes what they might have seen:

> Peddlers along New York's Sixth Avenue, their carts decorated with Christmas bells and sprays of holly, offered a variety of inexpensive machine-made toys-miniature upholstered furniture and tin soldiers…Buyers were mesmerized by demonstrations of mechanical elephants, camels and beetles. In the midst of the bazaar, Salvation Army soldiers, standing by their kettles, tried to reach the conscience and move the spirit with anthems of the season.[1]

The loud jangle of coins that Christmas shoppers dropped into the Salvation Army kettles encouraged Clifford and Lizzie to contribute the small change they had in their pockets. At the time they were both proud of their small gift, but as their income increased through the years, so did their contributions. Giving to the Salvation Army was to become a special family tradition that they maintained throughout their lives.

Clifford and Lizzie also enjoyed wandering into one of the many open churches along Fifth Avenue to enjoy the Christmas displays and to pray together silently. The colorful stained glass windows depicting various scenes from the Bible and the bountiful snow white and Christmas red poinsettias that were on display throughout the church—gladdened their hearts.

The Christmas holidays that Clifford and Lizzie shared in the city were memorable, and they savored each precious joy-filled moment they spent together. As the afternoons ran their course and the time came for each of them to go home, they would warmly embrace and agree that New York City had no equal for its advancement of the Christmas spirit.

Meeting Lizzie's Parents

Clifford spent many hours at Lizzie's home during the Christmas holidays and thereafter. He became increasingly comfortable in the company of her parents. He learned that her mother was Eliza Jane Squier, the daughter of George Squier and Charlotte Whitehead. She was born December 3, 1838, in Morris County, New Jersey. (She died in New York in 1929.) Lizzie's father was Henry Clay Adams. He was born on January 2, 1836, in New York City. (He died there on January 2,

1890.)[2] Henry had crossed the Atlantic from his native Scotland on a sailing sloop in 1826 to establish himself in a highly successful mercantile business.

Lizzie's parents were both first-generation Americans. Married on January 2, 1860, they went on to raise a family of eight children—three sons and five daughters—in New York City. One of those daughters was Elizabeth or "Lizzie" as she was affectionately known. She was born February 27, 1865, in Whippany, New Jersey.[3]

Lizzie's parents: Eliza Jane (Squier) Adams and Henry Adams

Henry Adams, with his brother, Robert, had been the highly successful co-owner and operator of R & H Adams, a manufacturer of beautiful silk and cotton goods with mills in Patterson, New Jersey, Birmingham, Connecticut, and North Scituate, Rhode Island. The mills in Patterson covered several city blocks. In the mid to late nineteenth century, these mills produced some three million pieces of mosquito netting a year, as well as very large quantities of crinoline, buckram, and about 2,000 pounds of silk per week. Many of these mills remain standing today: ghostlike and abandoned.

The Adams mills were recognized as the largest in the world exclusively devoted to that business. In fact, the mills were known to have produced more kinds of those products than all the other mills in the world combined. Orders came in from all over the continent. The community plants reportedly employed, directly or indirectly, several thousand persons.

Corporate offices, including the company's salesrooms for both the silk and cotton products were located at Numbers 14 and 16 Greene Street in New York City. Lizzie, who was known to have an exceptionally good head for numbers and who was skilled at customer relations, was employed in the company's New York office along with her brother, Clinton.

In 1879, after having bought out his brother's interest in the Patterson mills, Henry had become the sole owner of the mills, and the company's name was changed to Henry Adams. The Patterson mills operated about 35,000 spindles and 829 looms at that time. After Henry's death however, the Patterson mills were sold, and by 1910, all of them had ceased production.[4]

Partnership: Engagement and Marriage

Lizzie and Clifford's backgrounds may have been quite different, but the romance between them blossomed. They enjoyed each other's company, and they had lots to talk about when they got together, despite the fact that Clifford, the farm boy from Westfield, hailed from a family with a relatively modest income. He had had none of the experiences that Lizzie and her aristocratic family had enjoyed. In fact, Clifford had not traveled at all. His friends, except those at Harvard, were all from farming families with limited education. But Lizzie and Clifford did share the indissoluble bond of their exceptionally fine educations and even many of the same dreams and aspirations.

Granted, it was light years distance between life on the farm or Clifford's bedroll and makeshift home in the bookstore and Lizzie's luxurious brownstone home on ritzy East 63rd Street, but the disparity in backgrounds was never an apparent issue for Lizzie or her parents. Both of Lizzie's parents accepted Clifford for what he was and were confident that his ambition, character and loving heart would take him far.

On June 2, 1890, Lizzie's father, Henry Adams died unexpectedly at his home from a neurological condition. He was only fifty-four years old, and his sudden death dealt a devastating blow to all parties concerned. Although the family's grief was immeasurable, Lizzie and Clifford consoled each other. Clifford's loving presence during that time proved to be a great comfort to Lizzie and her family.

Three months later, Clifford presented Lizzie with a small platinum and diamond engagement ring from Tiffany's, the high fashion jewelry store on Union Square whose reputation as the standard of impeccable taste was unsurpassed. Given his strained financial state at the time, Clifford's decision to buy a Tiffany ring for Lizzie was probably foolhardy. But all of his apprehensions were quickly dissipated the moment he saw Lizzie's delighted reaction when she opened her Tiffany ring box.

"If this is a proposal, Mr. Noble," she said, "then my answer is a resounding yes."

Knowing that her father admired Clifford and would happily approve their marriage plans, Lizzie was eager to share Clifford's proposal with her delighted mother. That evening they all celebrated.

On January 7, 1892, at 5:00 in the evening, Gilbert Clifford Noble and Elizabeth Adams were married in an Episcopalian candlelight service at the Church of the Incarnation on Madison Avenue at 28th Street in New York City.

"Weddings were part of the connective tissue of New York society at the time, and a wedding in an Episcopal church was considered a sign of status.[5] The Noble wedding was described by many as the social event of the year. It was presided over by the Reverend Arthur Brooks, a Harvard honors graduate, the founder of Barnard College, and a twenty year rector of the Parish of the Church of the Incarnation."[6]

The Noble-Adams wedding announcement appeared in Westfield's *Times and Newsletter* on January 13, 1892:

> The bride wore white satin with point lace and Roman pearl trimming. Her bridesmaids: her sister, Mabel Adams and her niece, Ethyl Adams, preceded her into the church. The young girls were dressed in white silk (no doubt a product of the Adams' mills) and carried bouquets of white carnations. Arthur Noble, the groom's oldest brother was the groom's best man.

> The wedding was followed by a lavish, private, pink bridal dinner served by one of New York's best caterers in the bride's fashionable home that had been eloquently decorated in palms and ferns for the occasion.[7]

Clifford's entire family attended the wedding: his parents and his siblings, Howard, Julia, and Arthur. They were all jubilant about Clifford's choice of a bride. They had only met Lizzie once before, when Clifford had taken her to Westfield to meet the family for the first time. Although Andelucia privately harbored some practical reservations about the difference in their backgrounds and financial status, she and the other Nobles adored Lizzie. Given her charm and outgoing personality, it was difficult not to love her, and they warmly welcomed her into the family.

The Noble and Adams families seemed to meld together easily. They talked incessantly during and after the reception, and they continued to maintain a lasting affection for one another through the years.

Clifford and Lizzie decided to postpone their honeymoon in favor of a later trip to Europe (which they took in 1900). They said their farewells to friends and family and left the wedding reception early to spend some time together at their first new home, a suite of rooms at the Loring, a very fashionable, expensive hotel located at 74th Street and Boulevard. Within a matter of days, those rather posh accommodations were exchanged for a small, far less expensive apartment in the city.

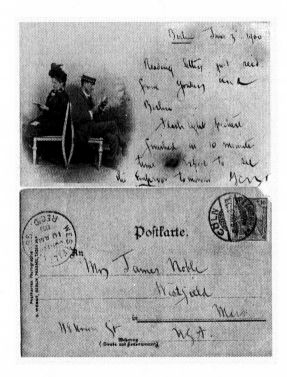

Clifford and Lizzie celebrated a belated European honeymoon in 1900. This postcard from Berlin, sent by Clifford to his mother, included their photographs.

The Hinds & Noble Partnership

As a new husband and soon-to-be family man, Clifford threw himself into the bookstore business with even greater vigor and enthusiasm. By 1894, two years after his marriage to Lizzie Adams and eight years after joining Arthur Hinds & Company, his hard work and creativity paid off. G. Clifford Noble became a full partner of Arthur Hinds and the firm's name was officially changed to Hinds & Noble.

Marriage: The Early Years

If the decade of the '90s had been a period of significant and positive changes for the nation and businesses, the turn of the century brought even more profound changes. Telephones arrived on the scene, and so did more functional and more practical automobiles. Modern coal stoves now warmed the households, bathtubs offered running water, and flush toilets replaced the annoying and inconvenient outhouses. Thousands of miles of railroad track and telephone and telegraph lines crisscrossed the country, and citizens everywhere were euphoric about things to come. Clifford and Lizzie looked forward to an exciting and prosperous new century, never dreaming at the time what phenomenal wonders, both good and bad, it would bring.

This was an especially significant period of positive change for Clifford. He was a family man and a partner in a prosperous business, with the days of too long work hours and camping out in the store long behind him. For him there was no looking back, but there were no regrets either.

As he no doubt described it to Lizzie, "Living at the bookstore was a sobering experience. The floor was hard and the word 'comfort' was no longer in my vocabulary. But you learn to do what you have to do. In fact, I had actually forgotten how comfortable one's home can be. But living in the store certainly made me appreciate the simple comforts that we take for granted. It was a painful learning experience, but one that provided me with a very strong foundation for succeeding in the bookselling business."

The first of Lizzie and Clifford's six children, Lloyd Adams Noble, was born in 1892 in New York City. But it didn't take long for Clifford to realize that the giant, booming metropolis that he and Lizzie had come to love was probably not the best place to raise a family.

Left to right: Kingsley, Lloyd and Kendrick, 1896.

And so, after much exploration and thoughtful consideration, Clifford moved his family north to the city of Yonkers.

10

Yonkers, New York

Clifford Noble's home at 441 North Broadway in Yonkers, New York.

Mrs. Malloy: You said you were from out of town.
Cornelius: Yes, we're from Yonkers.
Mrs. Malloy: Yonkers?
Cornelius: Yonkers; yes, Yonkers. You should know Yonkers, Mrs. Malloy. Hudson River; Palisades; drives; some say it's the most beautiful town in the world; that's what they say.
Mrs. Malloy: Is that so?
Cornelius (rises): Mrs. Malloy, if you ever had a Sunday free, we'd like to show you Yonkers. Y'know it's very historic, too.

—Thornton Wilder, *The Matchmaker*

◆   ◆   ◆

The decision to move from New York City to Yonkers was probably not too difficult a one for the Nobles to make. After all, Clifford's roots were in rural New England, and the natural beauty and serenity of similar surroundings were immensely appealing to him. As a near-perfect environment for raising a family, and with its close proximity to New York City, Yonkers satisfied Clifford's need for suburban life and community involvement and Lizzie's dream of raising her family in a simpler, more country-like setting.

Clifford and Lizzie moved to Yonkers in 1893, just twenty-one years after Yonkers had become a city and thirty-eight years after its incorporation.

"Yonkers is an old city, by United States standards[1] and can trace its origins to the mid-seventeenth century. It played many roles through its development phases: from its agricultural beginnings to that of a shipping port for local produce; then as an industrial center for immigrant workers, while a country weekend retreat for New York's wealthy industrialists; and more recently, as a suburb for commuters and middle class families desiring home ownership."[2] The greater majority of them commuted into New York City to work.

It is more than likely that when Clifford chose to relocate there, he was unaware of its unique history. But he was soon to learn, as Henry Brown wrote in his *Old Yonkers: 1646–1922* that Yonkers "began as an Indian settlement on the banks of the Hudson River and that it was the Indians who eventually sold their land in 1646, to Van der Donck, a Dutch settler, for whom the city was later named…The Djonk Herr's property (the young gentleman's property) was eventually contracted to 'the Younckers' and then to the Yonkers' and finally to just plain Yonkers."[3]

Because the city was strategically located about seventeen miles north of New York City along the Hudson River, Yonkers, with a population of about 13,000 at the end of the nineteenth century, served as a major corridor between New York City and northern New York State. From its beginnings, the city profited from the trade and commerce routed through its boundaries.[4]

It was the opening of the Hudson River Railroad in 1849 however, that contributed most to the development and expansion of the city's many industries. The railroad replaced the stagecoach and some of the steamboat lines that operated between New York and Albany. Philip Pistone reported on this happening and others in his book *Landmarks Lost and Found*:

> …The steamers were subject to the vagaries of the weather and could not be depended upon during the winter months when ice floes and heavy fog rendered the river un-navigable, and the coaches and buggies were slow moving

and dependent upon the health of the horses. The opening of the Hudson River Railroad in 1849 however, ensured a dependable means of transportation, thereby allowing for the development of the town's industries.[5]

...As Yonkers grew, large tracts of hitherto farmland around the town's industrial center were purchased by wealthy merchants and industrialists who commuted to work and sought refuge from the extensive urbanization that was taking place in the cities. Baronial homes set in park-like enclosures, with commanding views of the Hudson and the Palisades soon sprang up along North Broadway.[6]

(North Broadway, once known as the Albany Post Road, had for a long time served as the primary stage route between New York City and Albany.)

Clifford and Lizzie Noble's first home at Number 1 Shonnard Place was a small but comfortable brick residence located at the corner of North Broadway and Shonnard Terrace. It was there that Clifford and Lizzie's sons Gladwyn Kingsley and James Kendrick were born in 1894 and 1896 respectively. Clifford commuted to and from Manhattan each day, and the quiet neighborhood in Yonkers provided a welcome contrast to the big buildings, traffic, and hectic pace of the city.

The Purchase of 441

By 1911, Clifford and Lizzie had three more children: Constance Elizabeth, born in 1904; Stanley Rodman, born in 1905; and Vivien Thelma, born in 1909. So Clifford decided that their growing family needed more space. Clifford was now a full partner in both the Hinds & Noble bookselling business and the publishing firm of Hinds, Noble & Eldredge; the company that resulted from the earlier consolidation of the Hinds & Noble publishing company with a Philadelphia book house. So Clifford was doing quite well.

That year Clifford bought what was to become his family's permanent home: a four-story, red-brick, twenty-two-room Victorian house built in 1888. Located on an acre of land at the corner of North Broadway and Hudson Terrace. 441 North Broadway offered unobstructed, breathtaking views of the Hudson River and the Palisades from its interior windows and large covered porch.

Hudson Terrace had once marked the northern boundary of the village of Yonkers. Open fields and large estates occupied the land throughout the nineteenth century. In fact, in 1888 the first golf course in America was built just one block from the Nobles' home.

The builder of the Nobles new home had incorporated many accoutrements into the house for its original owner. These had been salvaged from a private estate in New York City owned by one of the nation's wealthiest families, thought to be the Vanderbilts or the Astors. That home, the owner of which chose to remain anonymous, had been razed to make way for new construction. Some of the trappings relocated into the Nobles' home included elaborate carved-wood ceilings and moldings and beautiful carved-wood fireplaces that were built into every primary room.

Clifford and Lizzie loved the house from the moment they saw it, and they affectionately named it simply "441." (By the late 1950s, however, that chic, very large mansion was no longer in style. Upkeep and utility payments had become far too costly, so the house, with many of its furnishings, was sold at well below market price and razed to make way for a multifamily development. Only the two impressive stone pillars that straddle the property's driveway entrance on North Broadway, with "441" still visible in black paint on each, remain.)

When one considers the imposing grandeur of 441, it seems safe to say that G. Clifford Noble had traveled an amazingly long way from the farm and from his humble existence at Arthur Hinds' bookstore to this lovely manor house on North Broadway. Family members today assume that its purchase was probably made possible by Lizzie's generous inheritance from her father although that has never been confirmed. But it must also be remembered that Clifford had worked hard and become a very successful businessman, so his income more than likely also played a major role in the purchase of 441.

Clifford moved his family into their new home in the fall of 1911. He would often recall that first morning, standing on his porch admiring the picturesque Hudson River with its many steamers making their way upriver to Albany. He enjoyed gazing at his beautiful, oversized yard, with its lush green carpet of grass and its many beautiful, mature trees—a very different environment than he had experienced in New York City.

Chestnuts and acorns that had fallen from the large old trees in the front yard dotted the ground, and chattering gray squirrels busily chased one another from tree to tree as they gathered the fallen nuts. With their cheeks full, the animals would scamper up the tree trunks to hide their newfound treasures for the long winter ahead and then return for more. The ubiquitous little gray sparrows kept busy below searching the yard for seed and insects, seemingly oblivious to the activity around them.

The graceful, overgrown maple tree at the center of the yard flaunted its best fall ensemble that year—a wondrous combination of crimson, amber, and pumpkin-colored leaves; an impressive welcome for the home's new occupants.

As he surveyed his property, Clifford couldn't help but compare his new residence to his cramped New York City apartment or even to the first small home that he and Lizzie had earlier shared in Yonkers. He knew that 441 would be a wonderful place to raise his family. And he was right. In fact, Clifford's children and grandchildren later used "441" to describe any place, quality, or destination that was homelike, comfortable, or totally suited to the lifestyle that they had cherished in Yonkers.

The crisp, invigorating fall weather, with its sixty-degree temperatures, offered a welcome respite from the sizzling hot temperatures and high humidity that typified New York City's summers. But even that steamy weather had finally run its course, much to the relief of all those who had endured it. Without the benefit of today's air-conditioning, city residents in Clifford's time simply learned to live with the heat which was tempered only by the fresh air and occasional breezes that came through their open windows.

With the summer behind them, the Nobles, who thought of themselves as being "out in the country," were now anxious to celebrate the arrival of fall, their favorite season of the year. Family members combed the many open-air produce markets in the nearby neighborhoods for the products of fall and returned with baskets of in-season vegetables, pots of colorful mums and chrysanthemums, and armfuls of bright orange pumpkins in various sizes that they ceremoniously placed on either side of their front door.

The Nobles all participated in the raking up and the burning of the many colorful leaves that had begun to blanket their lawn. They all enjoyed the sounds of the crackling flames and the tantalizing smell of freshly raked burning leaves that spread throughout their neighborhood; leaf burning was a hallowed autumn practice that persons in New England still seem to relish.

When the harsh winter blew in, covering the Hudson Terrace hillside with glistening white snow, the Noble children bundled up in their snowsuits and challenged one another to a downhill race on their makeshift sleds. Yonkers is a very hilly city, so there was never a shortage of places to sled. If Hudson Terrace or any of the other public streets had been shoveled and made navigable to horse and buggies or vehicles, the children would walk to any of several large nearby public parks. The parks were always crowded but lent themselves to memorable snowball fights, the building of whimsical snowmen, and several hours of sledding—many spent with their father, who often joined them astride his own sled.

The Boys' Rooms

One of the features of 441 that had fascinated Clifford from the start was its unusual three-story brick livery stable/garage, located along the driveway at the rear of the property. The basement and first floor of that building housed the family's horses and buggy and later their automobile. But the second floor featured four small, unadorned rooms, some with windows and some without, a built-in primitive desk-type work area with a stool, some shelves, and a bare light bulb that hung from the ceiling.

Clifford randomly assigned one room to each of his four sons. The boys were to use the rooms as their private think tanks, workshops, or laboratories. There they were free to pursue their own special interests; hobbies that would later translate into various remarkable and noteworthy endeavors. Kingsley Noble would later credit his early scientific experimentation in his room as having led to his becoming the PhD curator of the Departments of Herpetology and Experimental Biology at the American Museum of Natural History in New York City. Kendrick's early experiments with radio were equally impressive and resulted in his becoming one of the first crystal radio operators and first commercial radio operators in the nation (license number 199).

Clifford's assignment of the rooms was reflective of his lifelong commitment to teaching his sons the value and fun of pursuing their own creative, entrepreneurial activity. Despite the fact that his children described him as a strict disciplinarian, especially where the boys were concerned, Clifford generally let his sons choose the activities or experiments they wanted to pursue without comment or interference. The only exception was the few simple rules he imposed about safety and cleanliness. But he regularly dropped by to show interest in whatever they were doing and to encourage their efforts. Remnants of their respective activities, including a Morse code chart, a small scalpel and various instructional manuals, were readily evident on the worktables and bookshelves in their rooms, and they were still in place many years later when 441 was sold.

Residents of Yonkers

During the period when Clifford and his family lived in Yonkers, the community attracted an exceptionally large group of distinguished citizens. Many of them were neighbors and good friends of the Nobles and were frequent dinner guests in the Nobles' home. My father often told me about the dinners he attended as a young boy and the amazing and fascinating dinner guests that were there through the years. He was especially grateful to his father, Clifford, for making everyone feel important, and for his remarkable ability to lead and direct conversations so that everyone, from the youngest of children to the most distinguished of guests, was able to easily take part in the lively discussions.

Among the Nobles' many dinner guests was William Gibbs McAdoo. As president of the Hudson and Manhattan Railroad, McAdoo had built the first tunnel under the Hudson River. He was married to Woodrow Wilson's daughter. Dr. Elmer Sheets, who discovered Antiphlogistine and other medicines, was often there, along with William Ellsworth, president of the Century Company publishing house, whose publications included the famous *St. Nicholas for Boys and Girls*.

Other guests at 441 included Ellsworth Bunker, the United States Ambassador to India and later to South Vietnam; Charles Steinmetz, one of the world's great electrical geniuses; Rudolph Eickemeyer (who gave Steinmetz his start in America); Alexander Smith of carpet-making fame; and John Reid, who introduced the game of golf in Yonkers and who helped to found the St. Andrews Golf Club, the nation's oldest.

Edwin Armstrong, the father of modern radio broadcasting, reportedly dined at the Nobles', as did Norton Otis, whose elevators became an immediate success. The artistic realm was represented by the likes of James Renwick Brevoort, a prominent landscape painter of the Victorian era, and the renowned photographer Rudolph Eickemeyer Jr.

As noted in Mary Panzer's biography *In My Studio*, Rudolph Eickemeyer Jr. was a pioneer of pictorial photography whose landscapes and artistic portraits won countless international awards.[7] He was probably best known for his widely circulated photograph of the scandalous Evelyn Nesbit, *The Girl in the Red Velvet Swing*. She was the mistress of the world-renowned New York architect Stanford White, who was murdered by Nesbit's husband. The popular Broadway show *Ragtime* (1998), written by Tony Award–winning playwright Terrence McNally, retold part of her story.

When Eickemeyer Jr. died in 1932, his spectacular antique home furnishings were sold at auction, as was his collection of paintings by famous Hudson River School artists, whose works spanned the period from 1820–1870. At Clifford's insistence, Kendrick Noble's wife bought Eickemeyer's beautiful mahogany-cased McLachlin grandfather clock, with its eight-day strike and weight-driven brass movement. The nineteenth-century English clock, with its original purchase voucher and description, still stands resolutely in this author's home as a reminder of the fascinating roster of celebrities, inventors, artists, and businessmen who made their home in early Yonkers.

It was in Yonkers that Clifford and Lizzie raised their family. Three generations of Nobles were born and raised in Yonkers or nearby Bronxville. Clifford's children attended the local public grade schools. Some graduated from Yonkers High School and others from Halsted, a popular local private school. All of them went on to attend and graduate from some of the nation's most prestigious colleges and universities including Harvard, Columbia, and Cornell.

Over the years the Nobles were actively involved in the civic, social, religious, and political affairs of the Yonkers community and the surrounding area. Clifford served as vice president of the North Yonkers Citizens' Association. He was an active church member, a member of the Harvard Club, chairman of countless civic activities, and a member of the prestigious Amackassin Club that had been founded in 1888.

With its weather shingle siding and large indoor fireplace, the Amackassin Club was a popular site where members gathered to socialize and to discuss the affairs of the day. Located on Palisade Avenue within walking distance of the Nobles' home, the club was home to the second-oldest tennis facility in the country. It was there that Clifford was known to play a very competitive game of tennis and where his sons learned how to play tournament tennis. Stan, his youngest son, would later win many coveted national tennis championships.

11

Life with Father

Clifford relaxing with his book galleys.

To us, a family means putting your
arms around each other and being there.

—Former first lady Barbara Bush

◆　　　◆　　　◆

Clifford Noble always attached great importance to the role of home and family in his life, and he strove to make his domestic scene as well-managed,

orderly, and as happy as his business environment. Just as he took great pleasure in selling books and interacting with his customers, he also lived for the
affection and myriad rewards of his time at home with Lizzie and the children.

As a devoted husband and father, Clifford Noble reveled in his position as the
family patriarch. His move to Yonkers, and especially to 441, had allowed him to
establish a consistent, highly regulated family routine that everyone respected and
to which everyone rigidly adhered.

And if Clifford was lord of the manor, Lizzie was most certainly his lady.
Together they raised a harmonious and orderly family. Their children grew up with
a clear understanding that Father was the boss, and a believer in old-fashioned virtues, including hard work, faith in God, and rigorous abstention from liquor and
smoking.

Even with his sober reserve and methodical ways, Clifford created a loving
atmosphere at home. He adored his wife and children, and they adored him. He
demanded nothing of his children that he did not first demand of himself, and
within this balanced environment of love, discipline, and respect for one
another's talents, thoughts, and individualism, his children thrived.

Like many in his family, Clifford was not very demonstrative with his emotions, and he did not readily express affection in public. He resorted to humor
and a few warm hugs for the children and a loving smile and occasional wink for
Lizzie. But the children did not seem to need anything more; they all knew that
their father loved them dearly and was always there for them. In fact, Clifford
would freely admit to the contentment and pride he enjoyed in the presence of
his children.

Clifford was very much a highly focused, hands-on businessman. He felt that
personally reading and editing every manuscript prior to publication was one of
his primary responsibilities. It was also a job he loved. But the galleys that he
brought home in the evenings to be proofed were never allowed to constitute
more than a minor intrusion on the comfortable routine of his home life. His
family always took precedence.

Nevertheless, Clifford's children would sometimes describe him as being self-
disciplined to a fault. He knew what he wanted to accomplish, and he would
work diligently to get it done. But admittedly, he was not always tolerant of people unwilling to put forth their best efforts to do likewise. He believed that *trying*
to do your best was just as important as *being* the best. This valuable maxim
would be passed down through the generations.

Clifford Noble was a commuter who led a highly predictable and routine life. Early every weekday morning, he walked or was driven by horse and buggy to the Glenwood train station to catch the 6:00 train to New York. At midday, he took a short lunch break and walked to his favorite Child's Restaurant to order his usual baked apple. Each weekday evening, after a full day at the office, Clifford took the 5:25 train out of New York City's old Grand Central depot. That train was known as the "train deluxe of the road." First stop—Yonkers.

Clifford relished that thirty-minute ride because it gave him time to relax in a more-than-comfortable club car. As Henry Collins Brown reported in *Old Yonkers—1646–1922*, for a little more than $2.00 a month he could have his own private old hickory chair in this car, with plenty of room to move around in.[1] During the ride home, he chatted with friends or read some of the manuscripts that he was bringing home.

After replacing his horse and buggy with one of the new fangled gas powered automobiles, Clifford rarely walked to the Yonkers train station. Edward, his trusted and capable chauffeur and gardener, would meet the train and drive him to and from the station.

Mass production of automobiles began at the turn of the century, and by 1910, the entire country had entered an era of internal combustion. Clifford attended an automobile show at the old Madison Square Garden that year and was highly impressed by the vast array of horseless carriages with their hand-crank starters and shiny brass fittings. He was no doubt reminded of that chauffer-driven car that Lizzie's father had owned, one which he had so envied that day he met Lizzie at Central Park.

Clifford assumed that with all of its gadgetry, this new mode of transportation would not be embraced by everyone, but he considered it to be a challenge to the risk-taker he was. So despite the cost, Clifford purchased a Packard. Clifford was always careful with his money and not one to spend a dollar foolishly or without any forethought, but he apparently viewed the purchase of a car as a different matter. Few automobiles were sold in the earliest days. They were initially so scarce that driver's licenses were not required. Clifford wanted to be one of the pioneers in this fledgling industry.

Edward was also intrigued with the new automobile and delighted with the opportunity to chauffer the new purchase. He proved to be an excellent driver, devoted to Clifford and diligent about driving cautiously and in compliance with the prevailing speed limit. But staying within that limit—about eight miles per hour—was a daunting task, especially when one had to maneuver the roadways around buggies drawn by spirited horses. Newspapers at the time took great delight in detailing the arrests of "speeders," so Clifford made it perfectly clear that he would never tolerate being publicized as a lawbreaker. Pity poor Edward should that have ever occurred, but apparently it never did.

The moment Clifford arrived home in the evenings, noisy, excited, and adoring children would greet him at the door clamoring for his attention. Lizzie had meticulously timed dinner for his arrival. No one ever wanted to be late for dinner. Vivien, the baby and self-appointed herald of the family, would go into action as soon as she heard her father's car in the driveway. "Father's home! Father's home! Our dear, dear father's home!" she would shout. Although a bit melodramatic, the cherubic Vivien could count on getting her message heard. Clifford's nightly greeting was never too expressive, but the children made up for it with their boisterous, loving embraces.

Dinners at the Nobles

Not only were family dinners at the Noble household delicious, but the conversations, even without important guests, were equally memorable. Dinner was regularly served in the formal dining room on a beautiful old rectangular mahogany table. Clifford held court at the head of that table in a lovely Chippendale armchair, which he positioned next to the swinging door that separated the dining room from the kitchen. From this vantage point he could easily summon Mary, the family's beloved live-in housekeeper and cook.

Clifford also kept a long-handled silver dinner bell at his place. He rang the bell vigorously to call Mary or to summon a child who dared to be late for dinner. But the children rarely gave him that opportunity. Being late for dinner was not an option with him.

The dining room was the most formidable room in the house. The imposing brass chandelier that hung over the table with its large etched-glass chimneys, as well as the gas-lit sconces that hung on the walls, emitted a romantic glow that brought out the rich tones of the room's dark carved-wood paneling. With their chubby bow-hunting cherubs, the half-dozen or so carved-wood friezes that hung in both the dining room and library were of special interest to visitors.

Mary knew all of Clifford's food preferences, and those preferences dictated each night's menu. Clifford loved the appetizing smell of the pastries, pies, biscuits, and dinner rolls that Mary brought to the table fresh from the oven, as well as her traditional home-cooked meals. Clifford insisted that everything be freshly made, properly cooked, and piping hot. It's a wonder that the happy, unflappable Mary managed to accomplish such a task on a daily basis. Many years later, the children and grandchildren who had so often taken Mary's wonderful cooking for granted fervently wished she were still around to share her secret recipes.

Preparing and serving dinner to Clifford's standards was not always easy to accomplish. Because the Noble home had no electric refrigeration before 1913, Mary had to be chauffeured to the market every day to buy meat and fresh vegetables. The milkman delivered a daily supply of milk with his horse-drawn wagon, and the iceman delivered blocks of ice that were kept in the basement kitchen. Because there were no washing machines or dryers in the house, Mary always kept a big copper pot bubbling on the basement kitchen's coal stove for the daily washing of the table and bed linens.

A fresh white linen tablecloth, fine china, highly polished Tiffany silver flatware, and napkins neatly folded into engraved silver napkin rings—all wedding gifts from Lizzie's family—were prominent at the evening meal.

One may wonder how Clifford Noble became so thoroughly comfortable with this rather opulent lifestyle. During his formative years on the farm, he most certainly had not been exposed to the arcane world of the wealthy. It was Lizzie who was the unabashed expert at distinguishing between a salad fork and an oyster fork and between a finger bowl and a soup bowl, and it was she who expected her children to be equally adept. She believed that good manners implied good breeding. And Clifford rather enjoyed having the opportunity to teach his children all the social graces and proper table etiquette to which he had never been exposed in his youth. He honored Lizzie's family traditions and good taste, and he wanted his children to carry them on.

As soon as everyone was gathered at the table, napkins placed properly in their laps, Clifford would call on one of the children to say grace. They usually took turns because everyone knew Father's favorite prayer by heart.

"It's your turn tonight, Kendrick," Clifford would say, nodding to his third oldest son on Kendrick's appointed night.

After all had folded their hands and bowed their heads, the children, even the littlest, joined Kendrick in reciting the grace:

> *God is great and God is, good*
> *and we thank him for this food.*
> *By his hand must all be fed.*
> *Give us, Lord, our daily bread.*

The moment they finished the prayer, they all shouted loudly in unison, "Amen!" That was their standard secret signal to an amused Mary, who waited in the kitchen to begin serving the meal.

Although Clifford had very limited time for the children during the work-week, dinner conversation more than made up for that transgression. He encouraged each of his children to share their thoughts, even when notable guests were present. He had a wonderful way of listening and an uncanny ability to draw out his guests and his children and make them feel comfortable with one another.

Conversation included chats about the day's activities as well as discussions about the social, economic, and political issues of the day. The children genuinely loved being part of the grown-up conversation. They would later offer the same opportunity to their own children.

After dinner, Clifford gathered the family into the living room for family prayers. Then they assembled around the grand piano as Clifford played the popular songs and hymns of the day. Everyone, even the youngest, sang along. The songfest was followed by storytelling. The children would snuggle up in one of the living room's cozy, overstuffed chairs or on the lap of a parent or older sibling to listen to Lizzie or Clifford read their favorite stories. Mark Twain's *The Adventures of Tom Sawyer* and *The Adventures* of *Huckleberry Finn* were always requested. The boys, in particular, were fascinated by these stories, and their parents found it difficult to find a suitable place to stop reading for the evening.

An hour or so after this, Clifford would retire to the second floor to his large paneled study with its floor-to-ceiling bookshelves and hundreds of books. There he spent time working at his favorite old rolltop desk, reading manuscripts and editing galley proofs in preparation for their publication.

Once he had ensconced himself in his favorite three-cornered oak desk chair, with its well-worn arms and cane seat, Clifford worked until 10:00 PM sharp and then went to bed. This schedule never varied. The children respected Clifford's routine and rarely, if ever, interrupted him when he was engrossed in his books. From time to time, however, he would actively seek out some opinions from one or all of them on the topics covered by the manuscript he was reading—a "chore" they all competed with one another to take on.

Weekend Activities

Clifford presided over a strict routine for the family on nonschool days. Every Friday night he took all of the children to the local movie theater. The movies were nothing like the wide-screened color spectaculars we have today, but the children delighted in watching the black-and-white films. They loved the westerns, and they laughed uproariously at the Charlie Chaplin films.

As soon as they returned home, their father would encourage them to discuss the films they had seen. Those sessions often generated some hilarious but conflicting accounts of what the children had liked or what they had learned, making Clifford wonder out loud if they had all seen the same film. There was always lots of laughter and teasing, but the Nobles cherished this time they spent together.

Clifford with his youngest daughter.

Every Saturday, weather permitting, the family would gather for a picnic at a nearby park. Mary prepared the food, which generally included a tantalizing selection of fried chicken, carrot and celery sticks, deviled eggs, and Mary's "world's best" cookies. She packed these delights into a large straw picnic basket, along with cloth napkins and a freshly washed and pressed tablecloth, which Lizzie would spread upon the grass.

Once they had devoured the food, the children, including the youngest, organized a lively game of tag, hide and seek, or kickball. Clifford would officiate with Lizzie serving as the family's enthusiastic cheerleader.

Sundays were special days that were always reserved for worship—no excuses. Following Sunday school at the neighborhood Episcopal church, the children attended services.

The Noble family observed the Sabbath with strict devotion and reverence. Playing games or participating in any sports on Sunday was prohibited despite the fact that most of their friends were not subject to the same restrictions. But the children learned to cherish the day and used it to take leisurely walks along the city's aqueduct or to stay at home and read. Clifford encouraged his children to read the Bible so they could retell some of their favorite Bible stories at dinner that evening. They could also use the time to work on their hobbies or school assignments.

Clifford and Lizzie Noble may have run their home in a strict and disciplined manner, with rules to be followed, but the children knew exactly what was expected of them. They all discovered at an early age that because of the clearly defined limits and expectations their parents established, they had far more freedom and opportunity to pursue their own course than most of their friends did. The Noble children were all unusually bright and talented, and they all agreed later that the limits, almost paradoxically, empowered them to soar to their own greater heights.

12

Thanksgiving and Christmas

441 following a Christmas snowstorm, 1930s.

*And it was always said of him that he knew
how to keep Christmas well, if any man alive possessed
the knowledge.*

—Charles Dickens, *A Christmas Carol*

◆   ◆   ◆

> Holidays, when family and friends are gathered together, furnish some of our
> most cherished and enduring memories. Children, especially, are often both
> the subject and the repository of holiday memories that last a lifetime.

No one could ever be quite sure how many people would be present at a holiday
dinner at the Nobles' house. Friends, relatives, and sundry others were always welcome. Food was plentiful thanks to Mary, and Clifford and Lizzie heartily
embraced the old adage "the more the merrier." Their home was warm and inviting, and the family's open hearts attracted friends and others like a strong magnet.

Thanksgiving Tradition

Thanksgiving tradition at the Noble house meant a sumptuous meal served at a
festive table that Mary had decorated with colorful gourds, pumpkins, seasonal
flowers, and Lizzie's best crystal, silver, and china. Prayers preceded the meal.
After prayers there were individual recitations, both serious and hilarious, by the
children and guests about the things they were each most thankful for. Kendrick,
for example, once declared that he was thankful for finally having discovered
what a finger bowl was, and Stanley was thankful for not having been selected to
be an angel at the Christmas pageant.

Clifford's Thanksgiving declaration was always predictable. "I'm so thankful…" he'd begin.

"For us!" the children would finish. "You're so thankful for us, father, isn't
that so?" And Clifford would happily acknowledge their sentiment, his heart
overflowing with the love he felt for all of them.

Perfection best described the Thanksgiving feast at 441. It remains a foregone
conclusion among family members who have heard stories about Mary's meals
that no one, then or now, could possibly replicate her spectacular holiday menu,
although several have tried without success. Some say it was her unique choice of
seasonings. Others say it was the way she cooked the different dishes. Regardless
of one's opinion, everyone in the family did agree on one thing—Mary's real
secret lay with her passion and love for the Noble family. She simply loved to
cook for them. Most of the family acknowledges the fact that persons who cook
simply because it's their job cannot possibly hope to prepare the dishes that made
Mary so famous.

Thanksgiving dinner always began with prayers of thanks, usually led by Clifford. All those seated at the table held hands and thanked God for his many blessings. Whoever chose to do so then offered his own personal prayer.

Each family member had a favorite Thanksgiving dish that Mary would somehow faithfully prepare every year, regardless of how many different dishes she had to cook. And of course the oversized, perfectly roasted, and properly stuffed hen turkey was always the pièce de résistance.

Clifford loved making a production out of carving the bronze-skinned bird. The carving was followed by a call for all to pass him their plates. Each one at the table would voice his or her request for white or dark meat, and "lots of dressing."

Each year the children also vied for the turkey legs. Obviously two legs were never enough and that caused Clifford to wonder why some ingenious farmer hadn't remedied that dilemma. But he would always manage to resolve the problem, at least temporarily, by promising that those who did not get a leg that time would have one the following year. And the lucky twosome whose turn it was that year generally made it the first order of business to remind Clifford of his promise from the year before.

Once the drumsticks were served and the turkey was carved, Clifford would claim the wishbone. The tradition was that he would call on each of the children and guests to make a wish, if they so chose. Then he and Lizzie—in a highly charged, dramatic moment—would break the wishbone.

"Everyone make a wish. But don't you dare divulge it," Clifford would remind them. Then he would grasp one end of the v-shaped bone while Lizzie held the other. "If I get the longer end, all your wishes will come true," he told everyone. "But not so if your mother prevails!" he would add with a playful wink.

"Now, Clifford," Lizzie would say, gently rebuking her husband. Then, in a barely audible voice, and pretending that her husband couldn't hear, she would turn to her children with a broad smile. "You all know very well that it does not matter who draws the longer end," she would say. "Certainly the poor turkey can't play favorites, so *everyone's* wish *will* come true."

It was always a magical moment for the wide-eyed children, who eagerly watched the wishbone ceremony. Clifford, by some secret strategy, always managed to secure the larger end, and the children would clap and cheer.

To further delight their youngsters, Clifford and Lizzie hid shiny new coins at everyone's place—under the plate, water goblet, napkin, or silverware. The children were encouraged to save the money and use it as their offering in church. The amount of money increased gradually as the children grew older, and the tradition continued in later years as grandchildren became part of the Thanksgiving feast.

The Yuletide Celebration

As splendid as the Thanksgiving holiday proved to be for the Nobles, Christmas-time, according to all members of the family, was the most wondrous time of the year. Meaningful and lasting traditions abounded during the Christmas holiday.

Every year Mary invited several of her family members to help her prepare the lavish holiday meal. The women gathered in 441's large basement kitchen, from which they could sometimes be heard singing their favorite spirituals. Not surprisingly, the sound of the singing rarely failed to attract Clifford's attention. To the women's amusement and delight, he sometimes joined them in the basement and harmonized on a song or two.

At that time, many of the older New York and New England homes had a small first-floor kitchen that was used to prepare breakfast, lunch, and small family dinners. This kitchen could also be used as a service kitchen, much as butlers' pantries are used today for larger dinner parties and holiday meals. More elaborate meals, however, were usually cooked in the much larger basement kitchen and sent to the first-floor kitchen on a pulley-operated dumbwaiter.

The families that lived in these homes generally had maids or cooks who preferred to work undisturbed in the larger and quieter basement kitchen, especially when a meal required significant preparation and there were children in the family. (Incidentally, the dumbwaiter was a favorite hiding place during the children's raucous hide and seek games, so for more than one reason, the maids declared the basement off limits.)

A couple of weeks before Christmas Day, Clifford would gather the family together to hunt for the annual Christmas tree. Their job was to find a perfectly shaped ten-foot or taller Douglas fir—one that would not crowd the home's high ceilings, but full enough to make a statement in the room. Freshly cut trees were available throughout the city from the myriad vendors who hawked them on street corners and in the city's empty lots.

Getting eight independent thinkers to unanimously agree on the "perfect" tree was not always an easy task. Yet Clifford's finely tuned mediation skills somehow got the job done each year despite a few predictable tears from those who didn't get their way.

Clifford and Lizzie had a large collection of colorful glass Christmas tree ornaments that they had collected through the years. These were revered as tangible links to earlier celebrations. While Clifford and Lizzie carefully hung these in protected places, they also encouraged their children to add their own homemade touches to the tree. Delighting in the opportunity, the children often worked for weeks cutting, pasting, crafting, and then hanging their own paper ornaments on the tree. In some cases they added remnants of nature, such as the abandoned bird nest that Connie discovered one morning on the front lawn and carefully placed on the tree.

No one would have thought of missing the decorating of the Christmas tree. This was a cherished family tradition, a festive occasion to which friends and extended family were also invited. All were encouraged to add an ornament of their own—one they had either made or bought, but one that held special meaning for them.

During the cold Christmas holidays, when a roaring fire crackling in the hearth illuminated the eclectically decorated, radiant tree, the family, caught up in the joy of the moment, would frequently gather to spend time together and share stories.

It was at one of these times that Lizzie would retrieve the family's lovely old carved-wood Nativity scene from storage and lovingly place it atop the piano amidst some fresh evergreen she had borrowed from the tree. The crèche had been a favorite of her mother's, and it was now Lizzie's favorite as well.

It was family tradition to have the camels, the shepherds, Mary and Joseph, and the manger all carefully put in place prior to Christmas, but the wise men and the baby Jesus would not be added until Christmas morning. The effect was profoundly dramatic, and it never went unnoticed by the Noble children. In later years they would carry on the same tradition with their own families.

Clifford and Lizzie with five of their children.

And what would the Christmas celebration have been without the church Christmas pageant on Christmas Eve? The pageant was always the highlight of the season for families. The Noble children, regardless of age, were all encouraged to participate, and they did so willingly. In fact they often competed for parts: the angels, the shepherds, the wise men, and Mary and Joseph. Clifford believed that it was a good thing the minister cast the parts. That always averted a lot of unhappiness and sibling rivalry.

Once it was determined who would get what part, Lizzie worked for weeks sewing the costumes, using burlap bags for the shepherds' robes and cotton and silk remnants for the angels. Rehearsals were always lively affairs with lots of refreshments and teasing about who had been—or had not been—chosen for a particular role. The Noble boys were quite vocal about their refusal to be angels, and the minister must have wisely decided that they weren't right for those parts anyway.

Clifford kept his grand piano in the living room, and after the entire family attended the pageant and the early candlelit church service, they would walk home together through the deep drifts of newly fallen snow to a family Christmas carol fest.

Chilled from the biting cold, the shivering children would all rush to secure a spot before the blazing fireplace. They would warm themselves while chatting about the pageant and the forthcoming Christmas Day festivities.

The fireplace mantel, decorated with aromatic greenery, sported the children's hand-knit Christmas stockings, each personalized by Lizzie and just waiting to be filled by Santa.

Mistletoe tied in festive red and green ribbons hung over the doorways to the living room and library. Clifford's two daughters, Vivien and Constance, would studiously try to avoid passing beneath those traditional bouquets in order to dodge their playful father's kisses, while laughingly teasing him about his inability to catch them.

Christmas, like Thanksgiving, was a time for friends and extended family, who were all invited to join the festivities on Christmas Eve. As guests arrived, everyone gathered around the grand piano to sing their favorite Christmas carols while Clifford accompanied them. There they also sipped hot chocolate in brightly colored Christmas mugs and munched on Mary's assortment of delicious, fresh-baked Christmas cookies.

Following the songfest, the group assembled near the Christmas tree to hear Clifford read Charles Dickens's *A Christmas Carol*. When Clifford was through reading, Lizzie had everyone sign and date one of the pages of the book. She read from those pages every Christmas Eve to help everyone recall those friends and family members, some of them no longer living, who had been present at earlier holiday gatherings.

On Christmas morning Clifford and Lizzie would remain in bed, waiting for the children to summon them. Having stayed up very late the night before arranging the gifts from Santa Claus around the tree, they would always foolishly hope that they'd be allowed to sleep in, but that never happened.

Once awakened, Clifford and Lizzie, still in their bedclothes, would join the noisy and excited children as they scrambled down the winding staircase to have breakfast and open presents. Lizzie tried to encourage them to open their gifts slowly so she could record the givers for later thank-you notes, but that was usually a losing battle.

The homemade baked "surprises" and warm milk that the children had left for Santa Claus on Christmas Eve were always gone in the morning, causing a much relieved Vivien and Stan to shout, "He came!"

"Now maybe you'll believe us," said Lloyd and Kingsley. "There really is a Santa Claus." If the older children didn't believe in Santa Claus, they at least assured their younger siblings they did, for fear they would be eliminated from his gift list.

On Christmas morning the children found Santa Claus's gifts, along with presents from others, carefully arranged under the tree and tucked inside their stockings. The larger, unwrapped toys like bikes, large dolls, tea sets, and wagons were always the high points of Christmas morning, and the delighted shouts and giggles from the appreciative children who had found the gifts meant for them were almost deafening.

Every year during breakfast and prior to the opening of gifts, Clifford read the Christmas story from the Bible. The story was a bit sobering, especially with a room overflowing with presents, but as years passed and the children got older, they took turns reading the Christmas story and came to appreciate more and more the true meaning of Christmas.

Once the family had opened all their gifts, Clifford presided over his traditional command performance in the kitchen as he formally presented Mary with a generous bonus and a special Christmas gift which Lizzie had painstakingly wrapped in Christmas paper. That gift was likely to have been secured by some lovely silk ribbon Lizzie had preserved from her father's silk mills. She saved the silk for such special occasions as this.

"I do declare, Mary," an emotional Clifford would say in a different way each year, "we are all thankful to have you as part of our family. You're not only the world's best cook and housekeeper, you have also, more importantly, shared yourself and your love with all of us. We have all been richly blessed."

In her typical unhurried, selfless manner, Mary would thank Clifford and then share her affection for each of the Nobles, and her gratitude for allowing her to be part of the family. It was always a tearful occasion and, as Vivien would later say, "the best and most spirit-filled time of Christmas."

Of course, the favorite part of the day was most likely Mary's holiday feast. Mary's family helpmates in the basement would send the different dishes up to the first-floor kitchen, course by course, in the pots in which they had been cooked. Mary would transfer each selection to the family's most attractive silver serving pieces. Then, dressed in her crisp, immaculate black uniform with its white lace-trimmed collar and apron, she would serve the food to the appreciative family and their guests.

When dinner ended, so did the festivities for yet another year. With many warm hugs and tearful good-byes, well-fed, happy friends and relatives headed home, usually through drifts of falling snow. The lovely white snowflakes that quickly covered the ground in fairyland fashion provided a magical ending to a perfect Christmas day.

The Noble children all willingly helped with the cleanup. There were floors to sweep, Christmas wrapping paper to discard, ribbons to roll up for another year, toys to be carefully placed in their new owner's room, and dishes to hand wash and put away. Mary was given some time off to enjoy the remainder of Christmas and the following day with her family. The children were required to finish cleanup duty before they could play with their new toys. Clifford and his children worked as a team, laughing and sharing experiences of the season, and the chore was completed in no time at all.

Clifford was a master at motivating and inspiring others to achieve a common goal. He would empower them to accomplish disagreeable, tedious tasks, and even a few that would turn out to be surprisingly fun, by clarifying what was expected and how this might be best accomplished, and then becoming involved in the activity himself.

13

Vacations

The ferry arrives at Point O'Woods.

*Children will not remember you for the material things
you provided, but for the feeling that you cherished them.*

—Richard L. Evans
—Jack Canfield, *A 2nd Helping of Chicken Soup for the Soul*

◆   ◆   ◆

Clifford Noble demonstrated a total commitment to every aspect of his life, including his family's summer vacations. He immersed himself completely in his vacation retreat activities, and the joy-filled time he spent there with his family allowed him to replenish his energy and rejuvenate his spirit. What we know of those summer weekends with his beloved family inspires admiration—and perhaps a bit of envy.

If the term had existed in his day, G. Clifford Noble would have been the first to label himself a workaholic. His friends and family would have said the same thing. But Clifford was wise enough to know that if one were to maintain good health and well-being—as well as a happy and secure family—a stressful, hectic work schedule needed to be offset by goodly doses of joyous leisure time.

Because of his demanding work schedule, Clifford often had to indefinitely postpone plans to take his family on formal annual vacations. But Clifford understood that life was precious and fleeting. Taking time out from his busyness to enjoy his family needed to become his top priority. After all, having a successful business would matter little if he had not taken the time to share time and have fun with his loved ones.

And so, with a little prodding from his family, Clifford looked into the possibility of vacationing at a nearby retreat called Point O'Woods. The family had heard about the island retreat from friends who summered there, and they begged Clifford to give it a try. Clifford reluctantly agreed to rent a cottage for one month—"But *only* for one month," he told his wife and children emphatically.

As noted in a 1966 article from the *Fire Island Guide,* Point O'Woods was founded in 1890 when the Long Island Chautauqua Association purchased 600 acres of land on Fire Island as a summer retreat for its members and assumed the name "The Point O'Woods Association."[1]

This woodsy resort community lies across the Great South Bay from Bay Shore, New York, just fifty miles from New York City. The community is approximately one mile long and one-half-mile wide, and it is one of twenty or so unique communities located along a thirty-two mile stretch of white, unblemished beach along the Atlantic Ocean, on the sandy land mass known as Fire Island.

All the affairs of the community are run by the Point O'Woods Association, a private corporation whose stockholders are the home owners. The Association has never paid a dividend, but plows back any profits for further community development.

The Association owns all the land and all the facilities—the utilities, the dock and the public buildings. Each of the 120 homes are privately owned but they were built on a long term ground lease from the Association. The number of homes is held constant, although a few new ones have been built in recent years—to replace the nine oceanfront homes that were swept away by the 1962 hurricane…[1]

As the Point O'Woods Handbook declares, "Point O' Woods is a unique community. It is unique in appearance, unique in organization and unique in custom and tradition."[2]

Even today there are reportedly no paved streets and no motor vehicles at the resort, save for the few that are operated by the Point O'Woods Association to maintain services to the community. Residents access the island by pedestrian ferryboats that make regular runs between Bay Shore, New York, and Point O'Woods in accordance with a strict published schedule. Residents and guests alike leave their automobiles parked in one of the many commercial parking lots in Bay Shore, ready for the return trip to the city.

In Clifford's day, bicycles equipped with large straw baskets provided the only way, other than walking, for people to get around. Luggage was generally transported from the ferry by small, hand-pulled wooden wagons that local residents left at the ferry landing for guests or for family members or by the community's only small railroad—a gas powered engine and four flat cars that carry items from the bayside ferry dock to the Clubhouse.

The children of island residents who had arrived in Point O'Woods a week or so earlier often did the hauling of suitcases from the ferry by family-owned wagons. Meeting the ferryboat had long been a local tradition for youngsters, who could earn a few cents by pulling a luggage-filled wagon to the new arrival's home.

The community had, and probably still has, but one small grocery store, a candy store, a post office, a tennis club, a yacht club, and a nondenominational church. In Clifford Noble's time, the oceanfront also boasted the popular Club at Point O'Woods Inc. Its guest rooms and indoor and outdoor restaurants overlooking the Atlantic Ocean were the favorite retreat of local residents.

During his first vacation at Point O'Woods, in the summer of 1905, Clifford was energized by the smell of the salt air and captivated by the community's unpretentious charm. It was in Point O'Woods that he could experience a sense of happy abandon. Here was a retreat where he was incredibly happy and free; a place where he was able to reinvigorate the depths of his soul. And in no time at all he had completely fallen in love with the island.

Clifford loved to stroll along the boardwalks that traversed the community and connected the interior walkways with the cottages, the Club, the post office, the stores, and the stairways to the beach. More often than not he was accompanied by Lizzie and his children and later by his grandchildren. And it wasn't unusual to see a whole passel of adoring young children from other households also following in his wake.

The romantic, old-fashioned gas lights perched atop dark green wooden lampposts and placed at intervals along the walkways fascinated Clifford, as did the lonely old lamplighter who appeared at dusk each evening to light them.

The areas bordering the walkways and the open fields were laden with wild shrubbery and berry bushes, and Clifford and Lizzie would often stop to gather wild blueberries in small containers they had brought along. The family would later transform their harvest into a mouthwatering pie or cobbler.

During the weekday, island residents, dressed casually in colorful cotton shorts, summer dresses or bathing suits and cover ups, biked, or strolled down the walkways or headed for the beach. On Sundays, the men, dressed in colorful jackets, white shirts and ties, and the women dressed in silk print dresses, walked to the community's handsome, nondenominational church. The dress code, such as it was, was simply a matter of good taste and comfort.

Clifford lauded the strict Point O'Woods building code, which dictated that all cottages be built with a brown-shingled gabled look. Clifford considered that policy to be the perfect example of the virtues of zoning. It protected the community from unbridled development and ostentatious, individualistic display and made all residences consonant with other residential structures. It added to the unpretentious, private atmosphere revered by the residents, many of whom were prominent corporate executives or politicians, primarily from New England or other east coast communities, who treasured the solitude and anonymity they enjoyed at Point O'Woods.

Clifford also loved Point O'Woods' unique family atmosphere and its prevailing philosophy that children were an integral part of the community. In fact, Point O'Woods was so determinedly family oriented that only couples with children could rent cottages there, and that too only after being recommended by property owners and approved by a select committee. Families were required to rent a home for at least one year in order to be eligible to purchase a home.[3]

Point O'Woods was a conservative community to its very core; one in which the sale of liquor was strictly prohibited.

The Association maintained an outstanding summer schedule of daily activities for children of all ages, including day camp, sailing, tennis, crafts, and all kinds of sporting events. Clifford's athletic young sons were thrilled to see the many things they could do and were eager to participate. So the family was overjoyed (though not surprised) when Clifford, who had obviously forgotten his original "one month only" admonition, agreed to rent a home for the following two summers.

Cottage #134

In 1908, following a three-year rental experience that everyone in the family enjoyed, Clifford and Lizzie bought their own oceanfront home, Cottage #134.[4] Built in 1899, the Nobles' new summer refuge was one of twenty-nine such cottages constructed along the beachfront boardwalk. But "cottage" wasn't quite the right word for describing the Noble's large, multistory weathered shingled, gabled Victorian house.

Cottage #134 was especially unique because it was widely recognized as the only cottage on the island that was equipped with wireless radio. Clifford's son Kendrick saw to that, using the experience he had gained working in his room in 441's livery stable/garage. He spent a goodly share of his leisure hours building his wireless system and then sending what he would later acknowledge were the first wireless transmissions from Point O'Woods.

After their purchase, the Nobles arrived at Point O'Woods each Memorial Day to begin their long summer vacation, which typically lasted until Labor Day. Lizzie and the children would spend the entire summer at the cottage, and Clifford would commute to the island on weekends, returning to Yonkers on Sunday nights to ready himself for another week of work.

From its first- and second-floor porches, as well as from every room of their cottage, the Noble family could enjoy the spectacular views of the Atlantic Ocean, with its white-capped surf noisily breaking along the distant sandbar or on the sandy shore.

Lizzie cherished the time she spent on her upstairs oceanfront porch watching nature's show from her favorite rocking chair. She often got up in the morning before any of her family to enjoy the beauty of the morning sunrise over the ocean horizon. And once the family had awakened and had retreated to the beach, she loved to watch them cavorting in the ocean or sculpting sand castles on the beach as playful seagulls soared noisily overhead searching for food.

It was to this peaceful sanctuary at Point O'Woods that Clifford escaped each weekend to relax and to recharge his energy. It was also the place where he could share many hours of hallowed, uninterrupted, memorable time with his family.

Summers in Point O'Woods

"Lloyd, Kingsley, Kendrick, help me open the windows," Lizzie said to her three oldest boys, once they'd finished hauling the family luggage from the Point O'Woods ferry to their home and had changed into their summer togs.

It was Friday morning, and Clifford would be shutting down his office for the weekend and arriving on the ferry late that afternoon. Lizzie and the children had caught the early morning ferry that Memorial Day eve so they would have plenty of time to open up the house and ready it for Clifford's arrival.

Aerial View of Point O' Woods, N. Y.

"After being closed up for nine months," Lizzie reminded the youngsters, "this house needs a good airing! Connie, Stan, and Viv, you can help me remove all the dust covers from the furniture and shake out the rag rugs. Let's rid them of that sand that's been accumulating all year."

Lizzie stood in the center of the living room monitoring her children's progress, mentally ticking off the chores that needed to be done before the summer holiday could officially begin.

Lizzie always worked hard to have the home in perfect shape before Clifford set foot on the island. But when he arrived, he could always be counted on to organize the children and assign each of them unfinished jobs, many of which he helped with. They would wash windows, sweep rooms, clean and place the porch furniture, untangle the fishing pole lines, oil and rub down the bicycles and wagons to remove any accumulated rust, and in short, ready everything for the season.

These were chores that the entire family found distasteful, but they all knew that when the work was done, they would have the entire summer to do as they wished.

After Lizzie and the children had done all they could without Clifford's help, and after Lizzie had bought a few groceries from the local store and organized them in the kitchen's pantry, it was time to head for the dock.

Clifford Noble's beachfront "cottage" in foreground;
Kendrick's "cottage" in rear.

"Hurry, children," Lizzie called. "We must hurry down to the docks. The ferry will be arriving within the half hour!"

Little Vivien was the first one out the door, followed by her excited and boisterous older brothers and sister. Lizzie brought up the rear.

"Father is coming!" Viv shouted for all to hear, her little face flushed with excitement.

Lloyd, Kendrick, and Stan raced each other the few blocks to the dock, each pulling one of the family's little red wooden wagons. Although their father was only coming for the weekend, he usually brought more than his share of luggage. Besides, if other passengers needed help taking their bags to their homes, the Noble boys were ready to offer their services. They knew that deed would provide them with a good opportunity to earn some spending money and garner some appreciated recognition from the new arrivals.

As Lizzie and the children approached the bay, they could see the small white ferryboat slipping through the waves just a short distance away. The sturdy vessel nudged closer to shore, its railed deck crowded with excited passengers, mostly fathers arriving for the weekend. Stan was the first to spot his own father, Clifford, who was leaning on the boat's railing scanning the well-wishers on the dock in search of a familiar face.

"There he is!" Stan shouted, as he pointed at the crowds on the ferry. The children cheered. "I saw him first!" Stan exclaimed happily, teasing the others for not being as quick to identify their beloved passenger.

Lizzie laughed and joined her children as they all shouted their welcome and waved. They were delighted when Clifford, spotting them among the excited and noisy crowd, enthusiastically waved back.

Point O'Woods, without a doubt, was Clifford's Walden Pond and the family's summer paradise. Lizzie found it fascinating to watch the almost magical transformation of the rigid workaholic, who emerged from the ferry an entirely new person. Clifford could be counted on to quickly remove his jacket and tie and toss them over his shoulder before heading down the gangplank. Once he was on the dock, he wasted no time greeting everyone with warm hugs. The family would later recall how relaxed he always seemed and how loving he was once he reached the island. His greetings bore absolutely no resemblance to the formal, austere greetings he offered his children in Yonkers each night when he returned from work, and the Nobles all loved it.

Clifford could also be counted on to disembark the ferry with bags full of toys and candy for the children. There was something for everyone. The youngsters, even those who were not members of the family, made a game of trying to guess what he had brought that week. Clifford never failed to share what he had with all of them. There were jacks, kites, cards, dominoes, balls, candy, and other items, and all the children would join the Nobles in welcoming Clifford to Point O'Woods with clapping and cheers. Newcomers to the island must have wondered who this celebrity was who was attracting all this attention.

The Point O'Woods Yacht Club

Once on the island, Clifford never seemed to slow down. His favorite destination was the Point O'Woods Yacht Club, the very first place he would visit once the Nobles' home was made ready for the summer.

The Yacht Club, with its shingle-style architecture, was rebuilt in 1927 in its former location overlooking the Great South Bay. It was one of the more popular places for Point O'Woods residents because it housed the well-stocked community library. It was also the place where boat enthusiasts of all ages gathered for sailing lessons or competitive racing events. Most families had their own rowboat or sailboat, or they borrowed one of the sailboats the club used as teaching and racing class vessels. The Noble boys used the club's boats for races. All four of the Noble boys loved to sail, and whenever a club boat was available, they were ready to participate in the Yacht Squadron's racing competition. Clifford often joined them.

The Noble sons participate in the *Yacht Club sponsored tub races.*

The Squadron sponsored water sports of all descriptions. Its annual summer Water Carnival featured a tub race that was everyone's favorite. As soon as they were old enough, the Noble boys competed. Each race contestant had to use a metal washtub. Tubs were still relatively commonplace because there were no electric washing machines on the island at the time. The contestants could decorate their tubs as they wished. Once the race started, they launched their tubs out into the water and kept them afloat and on course by vigorously kicking their feet and paddling with their arms. It was more difficult than it appeared, and the first one to reach the finish line won, amidst the cheers of the appreciative crowd gathered to watch the race.

One summer the local photographer happened to snap a picture of the tub race. The photo later appeared on one of Point O'Woods' popular scenic postcards. Clifford sent one of the cards to his parents in Westfield, with hand-drawn arrows pointing to the barely distinguishable ten-year-old Kendrick in his tub. A handwritten message on the back side proudly noted, "Kendrick won that race."

Saturday Evening Campfire Cookouts

Countless other fun activities filled the Nobles' summer days, but the family's favorite event was their Saturday evening campfire cookout. The children were assigned the job of retrieving some of the plentiful driftwood scattered on the beach. Once the wood was laid out in some orderly manner and lit, the children began cooking the hot dogs and marshmallows that were available in plentiful supply. Even the youngest were allowed to use one of the sticks they had found on the beach to skewer and cook a marshmallow or hot dog. The little children loved being able to do, all by themselves, what their older siblings and parents were doing. It was almost a rite of passage for them—one they would brag about throughout the winter.

As the sun drifted slowly beneath the horizon and the night grew increasingly dark and cool, the family huddled together on blankets they had spread out on the sand. Then Clifford would hold center stage with his outrageously scary ghost stories, complete with his own sound effects, which never failed to terrify the younger children. But the little ones would find reassuring comfort by snuggling in their parents' or older siblings' laps, or by covering their heads beneath the beach towels until the story ended. Despite the occasional scream or groan, some contrived for effect and others quite real, the children would all beg for more, and the ghost stories generally continued far into the night.

Sundays

Sundays were a very special day in Point O'Woods, despite the fact that they meant shedding comfortable casual clothes for more formal attire. But the Nobles regularly attended the community's only church service, as did most of the local residents.

Each year some well-known visiting minister was invited to spend all or part of his summer in Point O'Woods in exchange for providing weekday counseling, doing needed pastoral work, and conducting Sunday's interdenominational church service. The chosen minister was generally widely acclaimed in his home church and community, and more often than not he came highly recommended by one or more Point O'Woods residents. These clergymen were usually known for their preaching abilities, and their powerful and timely sermons were the talk of the community during the week. Even the Noble children found the sermons to be inspiring and interesting enough to get them to church each Sunday without complaint.

Church was usually followed by a delicious Sunday buffet lunch on the ocean-front porch at the Club. Guests sat at tables, protected from the sun by colorful umbrellas. The view was spectacular and the gentle salty breezes tempered the usual steamy summer temperatures. Food was always delicious and artfully served. Without a doubt, dinner at the Club was always the highpoint of the week.

Comely young coeds from some of the best North Eastern colleges served as waitresses. Each one had accepted a very low-salaried job and a small bedroom at the Club in exchange for an unforgettable summer experience in Point O'Woods.

The Club at Point O'Woods—1931.

The coeds were always great favorites among the locals and especially among their teenage sons, who would occasionally conjure up sufficient courage to ask one of the female students for a date. Dates, by the way, were discouraged.

Given the absence of any bars or nightspots in Point O'Woods, or even any liquor store, a "date" usually meant a swim, a tennis game, an ice cream cone at the drugstore, or a party in a resident's home. Once in a great while, a young couple might make their way through the community's locked gates to visit one of the other nearby beachfront communities, which had their own style of nightlife. These latter excursions, however, were definitely frowned upon, and were generally expressly forbidden by Point O'Woods parents.

In 1932, Clifford's son Kendrick purchased Cottage #133, a two-story oceanfront house in Point O'Woods style located right next door to Clifford's summer retreat.[4] This arrangement provided Clifford with constant special company and an onslaught of grandchildren each year.

Clifford was the Point O'Woods' Pied Piper. Children seemed to gravitate toward him wherever he went, and they would often follow him around all weekend long. He had a natural affinity for children, and he sought them out as gladly as they followed him. He took his boardwalk stroll with his family each evening dressed in his commodore uniform. A plaque and photograph of G. Clifford Noble wearing that attire still hangs in the Point O' Woods' Yacht Club's library, recognizing Clifford as the organization's first Commodore.

Changes at Point O'Woods

Point O'Woods was the kind of place that most people thought would never change. It was always considered to be a special place in time. But over the past fifty years or so, east coast storms and hurricanes have taken their toll, and the once very large sand dunes that used to protect the beachfront and inland homes have gradually eroded away. Some of the sand dunes have been totally destroyed, leaving many Point O'Woods' homes very vulnerable.

Beginning in 1962, several oceanfront homes were moved back from their foundations to higher ground, although a few remained without any protection from the dunes. Some of these homes, including Kendrick Noble's Cottage #133, were totally washed out to sea in the storm of November 1991.[5] The national media captured stunning footage of the pitiful, intact cottage bobbing up and down in the Atlantic Ocean, the unrelenting waves gradually destroying its structure. That unfortunate image lingers in the minds of many Nobles.

After Clifford's death, his youngest son, Stan, acquired Cottage #134, which had not been destroyed by the storms. In 1977, following Stan's death in Point

O'Woods, Stan's children inherited the house. They later sold it, and that cottage is no longer owned by members of the Noble family. Although precariously located without dunes to protect it, Cottage #134 courageously hangs on in stubborn defiance of the elements. It stands in bleak contrast to the memories of the summers that Clifford Noble and his family so enjoyed and is even reflective, some say, of Clifford's own resilient, sometimes obstinate character.

Commodore G. Clifford Noble,
Point O'Woods Yacht Club

Today, many people are saddened by the changes that have taken place in Point O'Woods—changes that include the demise of the dunes and the destruction of the beachfront boardwalk, the Club, and many of the oceanfront homes. But it's no matter; seasoned and eager new residents still come. Those who have waited out a long, stressful year in the city come to the secure and restful solitude of Point O'Woods. Many of these community devotees and old-timers return each year with their children and grandchildren to enjoy all the summer getaway has to offer. New families come for the first time with great expectations. Most of them have heard tales about the grand and halcyon splendor that was Point O'Woods in its heyday, and they enjoy sharing stories with one another.

For those families who no longer own property on the island and do not return to visit—those, like the Nobles, who are merely left with fond memories—Clifford's family has a favorite quotation. They borrowed it from a book by Ernest Hemingway, and substitute "Point O'Woods" for "Paris."

If you are lucky enough to have lived in [Point O'Woods] as a young man, then wherever you go for the rest of your life, it stays with you, for [Point O'Woods] is a moveable feast.[6]

14

The Founding of
Barnes & Noble

Within every adversity lies a slumbering possibility.

—*Dr. Robert H. Schuller*
—Jack Canfield, *Chicken Soup for the Christian Soul*

◆   ◆   ◆

By all accounts Clifford seemed able to keep his home life and family activities well separated from his business concerns. This was a balancing act that not everyone today can manage. This chapter covers a seventeen-year period of growth, consolidation, disappointment, adversity, deal making, opportunity, and success in the book business generally, and for Clifford Noble particularly. The wonder is that Clifford found any time for his family at all.

In the late 1890s and early 1900s, New York City experienced an unprecedented period of physical growth. "The Great Consolidation" period, which began in 1898, brought the five boroughs of Manhattan, the Bronx, Staten Island, Queens, and the former City of Brooklyn together to create a giant 359 square mile metropolis. "This was also an era of unprecedented growth which witnessed the construction of the city's first subway system—an engineering marvel that by 1904, provided citizens with high-speed underground transportation from City Hall to West 145th Street, via Grand Central and Times Square."[1]

As clocks struck midnight on December 31, 1899, and snow blanketed the ground causing deep drifts that blocked the trolley cars, the new century began. Many Americans had modern conveniences at the start of the twentieth century that they had not earlier dreamed possible and the papers predicted more to come. Many of these new contraptions, like flush toilets, hadn't made their way to Westfield yet but Clifford wrote home frequently to alert his parents about exciting things to come.

Clifford and Lizzie spent New Year's Eve at home that year, simply celebrating the joy of being with each other and their family, thankful for their many blessings and looking forward to all that the new century might have in store.

With the new century also came an amazing proliferation of books. "Not since the invention of printing itself had there been such an outpouring of books, with the development of steam presses, and the growth of education providing the impetus for printing in enormous quantities for the widest popular sale."[2]

But despite the opportunities for more sales, this was also a very difficult time for the small bookseller, like Hinds. His biggest difficulty lay with the struggle between publishers and booksellers who quibbled over a book's net price. Hinds learned that if he was to compete with the larger firms in the book trade, he would need to join the traveling salesman groups, which all had major territories to cover.

But he also realized that not only did he need more book titles to sell, but since his inventory primarily consisted of textbooks, like other textbook publishers, he needed to expand his list of authors to include those who were well-known and highly respected in the academic area. "Book companies called in 'experts' to develop and oversee these books. Usually they were university professors...In the textbook field, unsolicited manuscripts were discouraged and college travelers spent more time on campuses, obtaining new ideas for textbooks and the names of authorities to write them."[3]

The large publishing houses in New York and elsewhere had both the revenue and the contacts to be successful in this endeavor and could hire professionals to help. But Clifford Noble, representing Hinds & Noble, was successful too, even though he operated on a very limited budget. By calling upon his many academic contacts at Harvard and in the public schools of New York, he was able to identify a number of topics that would likely be taught in upcoming years. He then recruited authors to write books on these topics. The books resulted in significant sales for his company.

In order to expand Hinds & Noble's new publishing division, add additional textbooks to its list of publications, and sustain and extend its retail operation on West 15th Street, Clifford recommended that Hinds merge the publishing component of Hinds & Noble with a larger publishing house that complemented their efforts. He felt that it was imperative that the company expand and add titles to their limited inventory. With the enthusiastic support of his partner,

Clifford succeeded in attracting Eldredge Brothers, a well-known book publisher in Philadelphia that was engaged in a book-publishing business similar to Hinds & Noble's. The Eldredge Brothers were the publishers of the widely used Chase and Stuart's *New Latin Texts*; Hart's *Grammar, Composition and Rhetoric*; Gerson's *Geography*; and several other titles.

Hinds, Noble & Eldredge

In 1904 the owners of Eldredge Brothers and Hinds & Noble agreed to consolidate their publishing businesses into a single new publishing house named Hinds, Noble & Eldredge. The new publishing house was incorporated under the laws of the state of New York. The capital stock of the new business totaled $300,000.

The merger specifically excluded the Hinds & Noble school and college *bookstore* business; this operation continued under Clifford Noble's management as a separate and distinct entity with its original Hinds & Noble name. Consequently there were now two separate book firms: Hinds & Noble *and* Hinds, Noble & Eldredge.

The Eldredge Brothers merger gave the former Hinds & Noble publishing company a strong new presence and credibility in the Philadelphia public schools that they had not enjoyed before. The partnership also strengthened and expanded Hinds & Noble's book lines in many other fields. The new company continued to offer many of the more popular book titles published and copyrighted by Hinds & Noble earlier.

Hinds, Noble & Eldredge developed several new titles, including an enormously popular series of music books called *The Most Popular Music Series*. Clifford had compiled some of the books included in this series while he was still at Harvard. These books were being offered at a time when people loved to gather around their pianos at home to sing their favorite songs.

Over the next twelve years, Hinds, Noble & Eldredge's business expanded rapidly, although relationships between Clifford and his various partners became increasingly contentious. Disputes centered around the issue of who owned the controlling interest in the capital stock of the new company. It was Clifford's contention that he and Arthur Hinds held the majority of the company's stock; the other partners disagreed.

If Clifford and Arthur Hinds did *not* own the controlling interest, then they were obviously at a disadvantage when operating issues and stock distributions were being determined. Clifford believed that his original partnership with Hinds & Noble and the subsequent merger agreement had assured he would have the opportunity to purchase additional corporate stock. "What's right is right," he told his combative partners (although in a somewhat more colorful way). But they refused to reconsider the subject and Clifford took matters into his own hands.

In 1916, unable to resolve his disputed claims, Clifford, who had heretofore prided himself on his ability to successfully mediate corporate disagreements, filed suit against his partners in the New York district courts. But the court, following a thorough inquiry into the merger agreement, gave Clifford a stinging rebuke, claiming that he was seeking to change a written agreement that he had previously agreed to. The court thereby ruled against him and further claimed that if in fact a legitimate discrepancy in stock ownership ever did exist, then Clifford should have taken steps to enforce action earlier.

As a result of the court's surprise action, which had come in early 1917, and following Hinds' decision to retire because of poor health, a disheartened Clifford bought out Arthur Hinds' total interest in the Hinds & Noble bookstore. Clifford withdrew his participation and stock ownership in the Hinds, Noble & Eldredge publishing house and resigned his position as treasurer of that company's corporate board. As soon as he was compensated for his stock, the firm's name was changed to Hinds, Hayden & Eldredge. Arthur Hinds' son, Thomas Hinds, managed that business.

Lloyd Adams Noble Publishing

Although Clifford was understandably very discouraged, he soon began to realize that not getting what he wanted might have been a stroke of blessed good luck. He wasted no more time bemoaning the court action. In fact, he became quickly convinced that the judicial decision had actually opened up some exciting new possibilities for him.

Now the president and sole owner of the Hinds & Noble bookstore, Clifford, went to work developing a strategic plan for building the business, while overseeing his family publishing company.

Five years earlier, around 1912, Clifford's oldest son Lloyd had joined his father in the bookselling business. But the new Harvard honors graduate was interested only in helping his father establish a small, family-owned educational publishing business, one that would be totally independent of the bookstore that Clifford owned with Arthur Hinds. The new publishing house that the father-and-son team organized was named Lloyd Adams Noble Publishing, with offices at 31 West 15th Street in New York City.

Clifford hoped to entice his older brother Arthur to join Lloyd and him in the family's publishing business, but that was not to be. Arthur passed away unexpectedly in 1914.

During his first three years in the publishing business, Lloyd produced a number of best-selling children's books, including *Mother Goose Songs My Children Love* and *My Children's Robert Louis Stevenson Paint Book*. Lloyd Adams Publishing was rapidly becoming quite a profitable business.

Though Lloyd and Clifford were optimistic about the future of their book-publishing business, they found themselves in the middle of a tumultuous time in history. The company had begun operations just as war had broken out and started escalating throughout Europe. This first "World War," as it came to be called, was to continue for the next four years.

On August 2, 1917, President Woodrow Wilson, with the unanimous support of his cabinet, asked Congress to declare war with Germany. Over the next two years, as the war intensified, America expanded its army from 200,000 to over 4 million men.

World War I

Caught up in the patriotic fervor of the day, Lloyd Noble joined the army and turned over his growing book-publishing business to his father, who was already quite busy with his bookstore. Lloyd's final publication, *Shurter's Patriotic Selections,* a collection of stirring patriotic essays inspired by the war, was copyrighted in 1918.

In serious need of some help, Clifford tried to bring his third son, Kendrick, into the family business. But Kendrick volunteered for flight training in the newly formed United States Naval Air Force instead, and was later transferred to a Marine fighter and bomber group that saw combat in France.

The war years seriously affected the book industry. In fact, the "plight of the schoolbook publishers was acute in 1918 and growing worse. They were affected more than any other branch of the business. Textbooks, for example, were hit harder by the general increase in the expense of making books because their manufacturing costs was a larger percentage of the total selling price than other classes of books. Some publishers had postponed price increases, but in 1918, the full force of increased costs was bearing down on every title."[4]

As Wolfe reported in *The House of Appleton*:

> Printing supplies became difficult to purchase, the cost of paper tripled, and the cost of composition, electrotyping, presswork, and binding became excessive. In addition, a large percentage of the men employed in the business and those who otherwise might have been available to work had left to join the military. Wage increases resulting from labor shortages further inflated the cost of doing business. Because of the elevated cost of manpower and supplies, by 1918, the cost of manufacturing a book had risen 35 to 50 percent. Textbook publishers probably took the biggest hit.[5]

In *A History of Book Publishing in the United States, Vol. 11,* Tebbel wrote:

> A publisher's biggest challenge lay with the question of how to avoid price increases and how to recoup the remaining deficit in profits after prices were raised. Publishing houses met that challenge in various ways. Most curtailed their advertising, but some stopped hiring salesmen, and still others, (like Noble's firm), no longer distributed free book samples to would-be buyers. Some limited the number of new titles they were willing to publish. But to further exacerbate an already bad situation, the market for books continued to dwindle as increasing numbers of students joined the military service.[6]

Faced with the challenges associated with the war effort, Clifford Noble was finding it exceedingly difficult to single-handedly manage both his bookstore, Hinds & Noble, and his family's textbook publishing company. The stress of operating two major businesses was impacting his health causing him to explore better and easier ways to handle his growing businesses.

William Barnes Joins Clifford's Firm

Following a brief hospitalization, Clifford began to give some serious thought to inviting William Barnes, an established Chicago bookseller, to join him in the reorganization of his bookselling company. "A Brief History of Follett Corporation" outlines the company's history:

William was the son of an old friend, the late Reverend Charles Montgomery Barnes, who had opened a small bookstore business in his Wheaton, Illinois, home in 1873. Illness had forced the elder Barnes to leave the ministry, and the bookstore allowed him to pay debts and support his family. He used books from his personal library as his beginning stock.

In 1876, three years after its founding, Barnes moved his growing and profitable business to a small store on LaSalle Street, and later to Wabash Avenue, both in Chicago. From the Wabash Avenue location he sold books, stationery, and school supplies, and eventually expanded his company into the wholesale book business.

As Reverend Barnes's business prospered, his son William joined the growing company, and Charles Barnes became a recognized pioneer in the field of buying and selling new and used textbooks.

In 1893, following a severe recession, a new corporation was formed and controlling corporate interest passed from Charles Barnes to relatives of William's wife, Blanche Wilcox. The company's new name became the C. M. Barnes-Wilcox Company.

In 1902, upon Charles M. Barnes's retirement, William Barnes and John Wilcox, William's father-in-law, took over management of the company.

In 1917, William Barnes resigned from the company and moved to New York.[7]

The Establishment of Barnes & Noble

In the early months of 1917, Clifford Noble and William Barnes met in New York City to talk about Clifford's bookstore business and his plans to reorganize it. The two men had a great deal in common, and they seemed to share many of the same ideas. Moreover, they genuinely liked each other. For reasons not fully clear, Barnes agreed to immediately give up his executive position in Chicago to accept Clifford's invitation.

William Barnes returned to Chicago, tendered his resignation as head of the family company, and sold all of his shares of company stock to John Wilcox, who subsequently became company president. On January 15, 1918, that company's name was changed to J. W. Wilcox and Follett Company in recognition of Charles W. Follett, who had joined the company in 1901 and become a highly trusted employee.

When J. W. Wilcox died in 1923, Follett bought the remaining interest in the company. Two years later he brought his four sons into the business. Today the family-owned Follett Corporation, which began in 1873 in Charles Barnes's home, is one of the 500 largest private companies generating more than $2 billion in annual sales. Interestingly enough, this is the company that most often competes with Barnes & Noble for college bookstore business.

Within a week after William Barnes accepted Clifford's offer to join him in the reorganization of Hinds & Noble, the two entrepreneurs completed plans for their new bookselling business, and Barnes purchased one-half of the stock in the new company. Both men were very optimistic about what lay ahead. They agreed that whatever risks and challenges they would face, the opportunities before them were well worth it.

In the latter half of 1917, G. Clifford Noble and William Barnes officially incorporated the former Hinds & Noble bookstore under the name of Barnes & Noble, with Clifford serving as president. The new company began business as a wholesale book jobber supplying schools, colleges, libraries, and dealers.

15

Noble & Noble

The G. Clifford Noble family, 1931. Top row: Stan, Kingsley,
J. Kendrick. Bottom row: Clifford, Vivien, Lizzie, Lloyd, and Constance.

Nothing in the world can take the place of perseverance. Talent will not; nothing is more common than unsuccessful men with talent. Genius will not; unrewarded genius is almost a proverb. Persistence and determination alone are omnipotent.

—Calvin Coolidge

◆   ◆   ◆

Clifford's last great business venture began in 1921 when he formed the Noble & Noble Publishing Company with his son Kendrick. Clifford was not yet 60, and he was still filled with the enthusiasm and entrepreneurial spirit that had been the driving forces in his life. Even the Great Depression would cause only a temporary setback. Noble & Noble was a real family business and Clifford devoted all of his considerable energy and expertise to making the company a phenomenal success.

In 1919 after Lloyd joined the Army and left the Lloyd Adams Noble Publishing Company to his father to manage, Clifford was able to persuade his son Kendrick, who had just been honorably discharged from the Marines and was working with the export division of General Motors, to return to New York City to join him in the family textbook publishing company.

Clifford welcomed Kendrick into the firm in 1921, and the company's name was promptly changed to Noble & Noble Publishing Company. At the time, Clifford served as president of both Noble & Noble and Barnes & Noble. In 1924, William Barnes's son, John Wilcox Barnes, joined Barnes & Noble.

In 1925, a period which saw considerable European emigration to America, Noble & Noble entered the adult education field and published Bradshaw's *Americanization Questionnaire*, Moffet's *English for Foreigners*, and Rejall's *Thirty and One Reading Tests*. The company was one of the first to produce books for adult elementary education, and one of the first to produce remedial reading textbooks. By the end of the decade, Barnes & Noble had become actively involved in selling books, and Noble & Noble was moving ahead with the publication of its popular *Reynolds Readers*, *Required Literature*, and *Required Spelling* books, which were selling well to the New York public schools. The family publishing company began operations that would help it become a major national player, highly recognized among the small independent textbook-publishing houses.

In 1928, with his sons back in New York and available to join the Noble & Noble Publishing Company, Clifford leased space at 76 Fifth Avenue from Samuel Gabriel & Sons. His immediate neighbors were Ginn & Company and the Baker & Taylor Company.

The Great Depression

As World War I ended and the 1920s drew to a close, America began to experience an unprecedented period of real estate development and unbridled financial speculation. But the infamous decade of the twenties, rampant with free-spending investors, ended dramatically with the stock market crash of 1929. The crash and the devastating economic depression that ensued would inflict wholesale poverty and tragedy on people from all walks of life and at all levels of society. As hundreds of businesses failed or were forced to dramatically downsize, one-third of the entire workforce became unemployed. Thousands were forced to rely on food kitchens for their daily meals. The drop in wages for those who were fortunate enough to remain employed caused a major decline in the demand for consumer goods.[1]

John Tebbel offered his thoughts on the impact of the Depression on the book industry in *Between Covers:*[2]

> There was no hint of impending disaster in the spring of 1929 as the output of books for the first five months of the year showed a rapid increase in new titles. There was an air of euphoria among publishers as they surveyed the prospects of fall business. Then, abruptly came the disastrous events of October in Wall Street, and by the first of November, alarm had replaced jubilation in the book trade.

> Like many other businesses, publishing did not believe at first what was happening…As the crisis deepened, the wise men of the industry were asked their opinions, and they responded with words of reassurance…

> Harry Hansen, (the New York World Telegram book critic), reviewing the first Depression year at the end of 1930, observed that no publishing house had failed, although a few reorganized and book lists were unmistakably shorter, but among authors and publishers there appeared to be a firm conviction that the public would continue to buy books.[2]

In *The House of Appleton*, Gerald Wolfe notes: "No major publishing house went under during the Depression, but they were hit very hard. Labor forces at companies like Appleton's were cut by almost 60 percent. The demand for books plummeted as readers suddenly found themselves more concerned about finding nourishment for the body than for the mind."[3]

Liquidations of a few smaller publishing houses occurred, but Barnes & Noble and Noble & Noble, with their limited overhead and highly controlled operating costs, fared much better than the larger companies. But in 1930, as the New York skyline continued to change rapidly, Clifford Noble's steadfast commitment to his bookstore was changing as well.

Although book sales at Barnes & Noble continued to do remarkably well, Clifford was deeply concerned about the difficult days of the Depression. Worried about the future of his own family publishing business, he reluctantly decided, after much prayerful deliberation and discussion with his family, to sell his remaining interest in the Barnes & Noble bookstore to William R. Barnes and his son, John Wilcox Barnes.

Barnes & Noble: A Barnes Family Business

In 1932, the bookselling company that had become a Barnes family partnership opened a spacious new Barnes & Noble bookstore, complete with mezzanine and basement, at 105 Fifth Avenue, on the corner of Fifth Avenue and 18th Street. The new store boasted the largest sales of new and used school, college, and library books in the United States. Four decades later, that same Barnes & Noble store would become the hallowed flagship of today's company.

The Growth of Noble & Noble

It was also in 1932 that Noble & Noble Publishing Company leased the entire third floor at 76 Fifth Avenue to accommodate the company's rapid growth. The company's catalogue, *Educational Books We Publish,* featured more than five hundred titles ranging from children's books, reading aids, and song books to logic and mathematics books, supplementary and basic readers, and volumes in Latin, Greek, and German.

When their lease expired three years later in 1935, the newly incorporated and still expanding Noble & Noble moved to the Stuyvesant Building at 100 Fifth Avenue, where it occupied the entire sixth floor.

In the "Biographical Narrative" he prepared for his fiftieth Harvard class reunion, Clifford recalled that during the decade of the 1930s, more Noble & Noble publications were being used in the New York City public schools than publications of any other textbook company. One reason for Noble & Noble's success was that the company had been especially successful in recruiting highly respected educators from within the teaching and administrative ranks of the school district to write or edit new textbooks within their areas of expertise. Teachers and other school district personnel were far more likely to purchase textbooks written by an author they knew and respected than ones from strangers who may not have been familiar with the school district's curriculum.

Kendrick wrote many of the textbooks that the company offered to textbook adoption states. Securing state adoptions for one or more of his various publications generally led to sizable sales and substantial income for his company.

(Textbook adoption states are those states that use state adoption as its method for selecting the textbooks that are to be used in their states. Today there are twenty-two states that choose what textbooks may be used. School districts using state money to buy books within those states may only select books from their state's adopted list.)

Apart from the many state adoptions that the company secured, Noble & Noble could also trace its success to its commitment to publishing textbooks that vigorously complied with the New York City schools' course of study. In the case of the *Required Spelling* series, the City's board of education ordered more than one-half million copies for use in its public schools.

Clifford's sons, who were exceptionally familiar with the New York market and who had diligently stayed abreast of its trends, not only became officers in the company but also its best salesmen. Noble & Noble's phenomenal growth in the postwar, post-Depression period surprised even Clifford, although it should not have. Clifford provided the company and his sons with strong leadership and an ambitious corporate vision for the future with a solid plan for its achievement. The company was conducting business in all forty-eight states, and even carried on a sizable business in Canada and other foreign countries.

Clifford seemed to be in excellent health in the early to mid-1930s, and he was looking forward to the company's continued growth and profitability. He took very little time off from work. This concerned his sons, but they had finally become accustomed to his exhausting schedule, and they simply accepted that which they could not change.

In the spring of 1936, Clifford spent many weeks preparing for his fiftieth college reunion at Harvard. He studied the faces of his classmates in his class yearbook and telephoned some to encourage their attendance. But it was his absence at the reunion—and the reason for it—that shocked and saddened both classmates and faculty when they heard the tragic news.

16

The Passing of a Legend

Official Noble & Noble portrait
of company president Clifford Noble.

*I sometimes think a person's spirit is so strong
that it never completely leaves the Earth, but remains scattered
forever among all those who love him.*

—Chris Crandall
—Jack Canfield, *Chicken Soup for the Grandparent's Soul*

◆　　　◆　　　◆

Some say that a good man's greatest monument is the work he did in his life, the relationships he nurtured, and the changes he made in people's lives. By that standard, Clifford Noble's memorial is far more impressive than even the magnificent mausoleum he built for himself and his family or the companies that he founded. He understood, and made an effort to convey to those he loved, what really matters in life—and we can learn from his example.

G. Clifford Noble's unexpected death on June 6, 1936, at age seventy-two, on the eve of his long-awaited reunion in Cambridge, stunned his family and friends and deeply saddened his peers in the New York book industry.

Clifford and Lizzie had spent months planning trips to their respective fiftieth reunions at Harvard and Vassar. Because the reunions had been scheduled only two days apart, they'd planned to drive first to Poughkeepsie, New York, for Lizzie's reunion and then continue on to Cambridge, Massachusetts, to attend Clifford's.

But just before their scheduled departure, Clifford decided to remain at home. He told Lizzie that he was tired and preferred to rest, wanting to be in good health for his own celebration. Their son Kendrick offered to drive Lizzie to and from Poughkeepsie. He was a staunch Vassar College enthusiast who had been named for James Ryland Kendrick, the president of Vassar College during Lizzie's senior year. Kendrick Noble was later selected by Lizzie's classmates to be the official 1886 class baby. Another son, Kingsley, a Harvard graduate, offered to drive both Lizzie and Clifford to Cambridge. It was a perfect compromise, and one to which everyone wholeheartedly agreed.

So Lizzie, Kendrick, and Kendrick's seven-year-old son Kendrick Jr., whom the family affectionately called "Sonny," set out for Lizzie's reunion. The event would turn out to be a festive occasion that the three, regardless of age, wholeheartedly enjoyed.

On the day the trio was to return to Yonkers, several family members joined Clifford to welcome them home. Kendrick's silver gray sedan arrived, as expected, late that afternoon. As it reached the corner of Hudson Terrace and North Broadway, the threesome was greeted by the four-foot gray stone pillars, each marked with the large black numbers "441." The pillars stood as sentries on either side of the gated entrance guarding the winding gravel driveway leading up to the Nobles' home.

Clifford was the first one to acknowledge his returning family. He had heard the crunching of his son's tires on the gravel in the driveway, and he watched the three climb out of their car from his bedroom window. He wasted no time notifying the household of their arrival.

Lizzie, Kendrick, and Kendrick Jr. stepped through 441's beveled glass front door, into the vestibule and front hall where the family's old oak hat tree stood at attention, showcasing Clifford's fine collection of walking canes, umbrellas, and top hats. As the stately grandfather clock guarding the foot of the staircase struck four, the three climbed the stairway to the second floor where Clifford greeted them at his bedroom door.

"Welcome home!" Clifford said happily, looking relaxed in the chocolate brown flannel robe and brown and white striped cotton pajamas that Lizzie had bought him for his reunion. On his feet he wore his favorite old dog-eared leather slippers.

But no sooner had he welcomed his family home than he grabbed his chest, fell clumsily to the floor, and lay motionless on his stomach.

"Father!" Kendrick cried. He rushed to his father's aid and felt for a pulse. Not finding one, he frantically called out to his father's housekeeper. "Mary, quickly! Call the doctor!" The rest of the family crowded the stairway and looked on in shock and disbelief. There had been no warning at all of this tragic happening. In fact, Clifford had looked quite well, and he had seemed to be in the best of spirits just a few moments earlier.

The family physician arrived and tried to revive Clifford, but his efforts at resuscitation failed. Just a few minutes past four o'clock that afternoon, the doctor told a grieving family that Clifford had died of a massive heart attack. The items on the bureau next to Clifford's chair indicated that he had spent a leisurely day preparing for his reunion. There lay his Harvard Class of '86 reunion badge, a copy of the class songbook, and the pictorial directory of his classmates that he had been studying in an effort to make sure that he was able to recognize them.

Clifford's death came as a great shock to the family. Although everyone in the room was stunned by the physician's final pronouncement, Kendrick seemed most affected. He had worked closely with his father after Clifford had sold his Barnes & Noble stock to William Barnes. The thought that he'd be the one to have full responsibility for the family business, as well as responsibility for the care of his aging mother, must have been an overwhelming prospect. He had also been extremely close to his father and had depended on him for advice and counsel on a variety of issues. Losing his cherished mentor so unexpectedly was an unbearable tragedy.

Kendrick had stood by in silent disbelief as the doctor struggled to revive his father. Then, without warning, the family member who was viewed as "always in charge" had fainted, collapsing on the floor much as Clifford had done just moments before. A collective gasp rippled through the family, who thought a second tragedy had just occurred. But the doctor quickly revived Kendrick, who was back in control in a matter of minutes, a bit embarrassed and still visibly shaken.

Lizzie, far too grief stricken and upset to be of much help, allowed the physician to call the funeral home.

News of Clifford Noble's death spread rapidly. Not only did his passing have a profound impact on his family, it was also felt deeply by the Yonkers and Point O'Woods communities and by the principals of the bookselling industry nationwide who had held him in such high esteem.

Funeral and Burial

The Clifford Noble mausoleum at Kensico Cemetery.

Funeral services were held a couple of days later at St. Paul's Episcopal Church in Yonkers. The church overflowed with well-wishers and mourners. During the service, the organist played *Amazing Grace* and *Rock of Ages*, two of Clifford's favorite hymns. The family's minister conducted the service. He gave a brief but moving eulogy about Clifford's devotion to his family, church, and community. "So many people *admired* Clifford for what he *did* with his life," the minister said, "but they *loved* him for *who* and *what* he was."

Following the service, a large black hearse transported Clifford's body to Kensico Cemetery in the tiny rural community of Valhalla, New York. A seemingly endless stream of cars followed behind. Within an hour the family and scores of mourners had gathered at the well-maintained parklike cemetery, with its rolling hills and magnificent mausoleums.

Kensico is one of New York State's most beautiful and popular not-for-profit nonsectarian cemeteries. Such notables as Tommy Dorsey, David Sarnoff, Danny Kaye, Lou and Eleanor Gehrig, Billy Burke and Florenz Ziegfeld, John Andrus, and many other well-known personalities are buried there.

G. Clifford Noble was laid to rest in a polished crypt within a large and beautiful stone mausoleum. The mausoleum stands on a site near the top of Iroquois Road (Lot #9015, Section 57), from where it overlooks the lovely surrounding countryside. There are stone benches on either side of the stately structure, and the name NOBLE, inscribed over the imposing metal-and-glass door, boldly identifies its occupants.

Several years earlier, Clifford had spent considerable time selecting the perfect site for the mausoleum and overseeing construction of the monument that was to entomb his entire immediate family. Funds generated from the sale of his stock in Barnes & Noble were used to purchase the site and construct the mausoleum. James Noble's decision to build a similar but smaller monument in Westfield's Pine Hill Cemetery had no doubt influenced Clifford's decision to build his own. The Westfield mausoleum currently shelters the remains of Clifford's parents and those of some other members of his immediate family.

Clifford had also commissioned the design of a beautiful stained-glass window, which was installed in the center rear wall of the mausoleum. The window depicts Jesus kneeling in the garden of Gethsemane. When the late afternoon sun streams through the window and lights up the mausoleum's entire interior, the effect is awesome. It is as if the heavens have opened up and chosen to glorify the loved ones interred there.

There have been many efforts by journalists and cemetery staff elsewhere to claim that Clifford's remains lie in places other than Kensico. One article, written by Jack Barth, which appeared in the June 1988 issue of the New York magazine *Spy*, reported that among the celebrities buried at Green-Wood Cemetery in Brooklyn, New York, were both founders of the company that still retains their names: Mr. Barnes and Mr. Noble.[1]

That presumptuous article prompted attorney Anne R. Noble, Clifford's great-granddaughter, to write in a letter to the magazine's editor (October, 1988), "While I have no information about the final resting place of Barnes, I can assure you that the *Noble* of Barnes & Noble was originally interred—and remains—at Kensico Cemetery in Valhalla, New York. Gilbert Clifford Noble, my great-grandfather, built for himself, his wife and their six children a mausoleum at that cemetery more than fifty years ago. I have placed wreaths there on holidays since I was a child, and can state for a fact that Mr. Noble never was, and is not, in Brooklyn, although I am equally certain he held no ill will toward the borough."[2]

To this, the editor of Spy glibly replied: "Green-Wood employees have twice assured *Spy* that Barnes and Noble are buried there in adjacent plots. We trust this is a case of misinformation, not disinterment."[3]

Lizzie Noble

Very soon after Clifford's death, Lizzie's children helped her relocate to a modest home at 44 Oxford Street in Montclair, New Jersey. She wanted to be near her youngest daughter Vivien, and Vivien's family.

Lizzie Adams Noble, 1930s

Lizzie became quite immobile in her later years, but the ever-faithful Mary remained by her side for the remainder of Lizzie's life. Lizzie lived to be ninety years old and died in 1955 at her New Jersey home.

Ironically, Lizzie's beloved gold watch, which she kept by her bedside, permanently stopped on the day of her death. It was studded with a single diamond and globes of rubies and sapphires dangling from a gold chain. Her father had given her the watch in 1882 when she entered Vassar College. She had worn it on her wedding day and never parted with it except for periodic cleaning. It kept perfect time and had ticked away the passages of her life for seventy-three years, ending its own life at her passing.

17

The Legacy

*Clifford celebrates this author's second
birthday in Point O'Woods.*

*Each of us leaves a thumbprint on the world, a record that we were here and who we
were and what we did. Your only choice is what kind of thumbprint to leave.*

—Sidney B. Simon
—Jack Canfield, *Chicken Soup for the Grandparent's Soul*

◆   ◆   ◆

G. Clifford Noble did more than establish the original Barnes & Noble and Noble & Noble book companies. He was an exemplar of Yankee determination, faith-based initiative, and creative entrepreneurship. He was a kind and loving man with a deep religious commitment.

Clifford left us with ten tenets to live by, a legacy that may inspire others to lead fuller, happier, and more productive lives.

1. Know where you want to go. Be passionate about that dream, and do what is necessary to achieve it. Keep the big idea the Big Idea.

2. Act. Goals and ideas are nothing without action.

3. Don't be afraid to take risks. Great achievements involve great risks.

4. Learn from your failures and mistakes. If you don't always get your way, consider that may be a stroke of good luck.

5. Learn to recognize good opportunities; opportunities can often be found in the most unlikely places. Create them where there seems to be none.

6. Have fun, love what you do, and smile a lot. Don't take yourself too seriously.

7. Be receptive to change and new ideas, but don't sacrifice your integrity or values. Think success not failure, but manage your time and money well.

8. Lead your life in strict accordance with these priorities: your faith, your family, your work—and in that order.

9. Let your spouse and children know they are cherished. Share joy-filled time with them.

10. Create a loving atmosphere in your home and workplace, one in which your confidence in and respect for others empowers them to achieve *their* dreams.

Postscript: Reorganization and Renewal

I do not know of any bookstore amounting to anything that cannot
be traced back to a single dominant personality.

—Lawrence Clark Powell

In the year following Clifford's unexpected death, Clifford's son Kendrick was elected Noble & Noble company president, chief executive officer, and treasurer. Clifford's youngest son, Stan, was elected company vice president, and Miss Anna C. Brehm became the corporation's new secretary.

Lloyd, Clifford's eldest son, had been forced to retire from the company earlier over a serious dispute with his father involving a personal matter. He had accepted a position as superintendent of construction for the Morse Dry Dock & Repair Company of Brooklyn, but after his father's death, Lloyd's brothers elected him to the corporation's board of directors.

With new officers in place, Noble & Noble Publishers continued operations from its offices at 100 Fifth Avenue in Manhattan. The company's 1937 catalogue was dedicated to Clifford's memory.

The December 7, 1941, Japanese attack on Pearl Harbor heralded the beginning of U.S. involvement in World War II. Thanks to the uncertainty caused by wartime personnel displacements in 1942, the publishing industry experienced significant changes. Many of the industry's employees were going off to war or finding work in defense factories. Readers were doing likewise. Many bookmaking materials, especially paper, became increasingly scarce. When materials could be acquired, frequent delays in shipment and delivery caused further difficulties and setbacks. As a result, publishing costs soared. To offset these elevated costs, publishers had to increase book prices.

When the war ended in 1945, Noble & Noble Publishers Inc. began its final twenty years as an independent textbook publisher. Under the GI Bill, millions of veterans returned to school, generating the need for tens of millions of textbooks and reference books. For Noble & Noble and other publishers who had established education departments, this brought a wave of sudden prosperity.

During the two decades after the war, Noble & Noble expanded its inventory. In addition to the books it prepared specifically for the New York City market, the company published a diverse selection of titles, including a number of adult elementary education and remedial reading textbooks.

Noble & Noble's enormously popular handwriting system, the *Better Handwriting For You* series, on which Kendrick Noble served as senior author and editor, quickly overtook all competitors. Twenty-four of the twenty-six states that had approved state adoptions, including California and Texas, adopted the series. This was an achievement that had not been surpassed by any other company in any subject area.

In the mid-1950s, in need of more room to accommodate a growing business, Noble & Noble moved its publishing operation to 67 Irving Place. J. Kendrick Noble Jr.—a former Princeton student, a 1950 graduate of the United States Naval Academy, and a commander in the United States Navy—joined the company as an executive vice president in 1957. His wife, educator Norma Jean Noble, was hired as an educational consultant, and this author was employed as the company's editor and sales manager in Texas to secure state textbook adoptions. A few years later, in the mid-1960s, the company moved to its final location, 750 Third Avenue in New York City.

By May of 1965, Noble & Noble had become widely recognized as one of the most successful independently owned textbook publishers. But the whole concept of educational publishing was changing. Textbooks prepared by committees working under federal and foundation grants of millions of dollars began to infiltrate the market. To compete in this new field, the company felt it would do much better if it merged with a larger company that could supply financial aid and additional employees as well as computer services and other logistical support. After researching the entire field, Noble & Noble started negotiations with the Dell Publishing Company, one of the world's largest publishers of paperback books. In many subject areas, paperbacks were rapidly taking the place of the more expensive hardcover books.

A 1965 *New York Times* article announced that Dell had acquired the stock of Noble & Noble Publishers Inc. Noble & Noble began to operate as a separate, wholly owned subsidiary.[1] Under this arrangement, Noble & Noble was able to continue to expand into some of the newer fields, such as programmed texts and paperback educational texts. The company maintained independent operations at 67 Irving Place for a few years thereafter.

In the years following Dell's purchase and eventual sale of Noble & Noble, several Noble & Noble bookplates and manuscripts were acquired by an impressive list of publishers, including Doubleday & Company, Bowmar Publishing Company, Macmillan, and, most recently, McGraw Hill. This meant that the new owners had the right to publish titles that were previously owned and published solely by Noble & Noble. That such acquisitions were eagerly sought is a testimonial to the quality and reputation of Noble & Noble's products.

Today, nearly four decades after the company was sold to Dell, some of the Noble & Noble manuscripts continue to be published under their new owners' names. These books generate relatively impressive sales to this day. Although all Nobles who had been senior executives with the company are deceased, the legacy that G. Clifford Noble left behind continues.

Barnes & Noble Lives On

In 1931, after Clifford sold his full interest in Barnes & Noble, the company, now under the ownership and management of William R. Barnes and his son John, initiated a publishing division with its famous and immensely popular *College Outline* series. By 1949, sixty-five of these titles were selling in a price range from seventy-five cents to a $1.50 per copy.

Years earlier, Barnes & Noble had acquired publishing rights to a number of book titles from Hinds, Hayden & Eldredge, which, according to Tebbel in *A History of Book Publishing in the United States*, Vol. 111, "retained its identity after the 1925 sale; a transaction involving mainly a transfer of titles, including the twenty-five volumes of Chase and Stewart's *New Latin Texts* and thirty-two volumes of *Pearson's Speaker Series*."[2] These titles and others allowed the company to enjoy decades of profitability as both bookseller and book publisher.

By the 1960s, Barnes & Noble held interests in numerous components of the book industry, but the majority of its revenue still came from textbook sales. A 42,000-square-foot bookstore and storage space at Fifth Avenue and 18th Street, a mile north of the New York University neighborhood, provided the company's main venue for retail sales.

The company had become increasingly profitable as both bookseller and book publisher during the Depression years, and it would continue to be profitable for the next three decades despite the fact that the bookselling business was largely dominated by department-store book departments and independent mom-and-pop stores. Brentano's, a new book retailer, was the company's primary competition. But Barnes & Noble prospered by selling textbooks and technical books as well as a very large selection of general interest titles.

Although the business was lucrative at the time, misfortune struck when John Barnes, William Barnes's son and partner, died in 1969. With no other family members available to take over, Barnes sold the company to Amtel, a publicly traded retail conglomerate. During this period it was popular for large conglomerates to acquire sundry unrelated businesses about which they knew little, and Amtel was no exception. After a year of trying to maintain profitability and failing, the conglomerate reportedly offered the business to a member of the Follett family who was skeptical that a bookstore and wholesale business in New York City, at the time, could have a stable future. Consequently, the Follett family member refused the offer.

By 1971, Amtel had concluded that the business was in a long-term decline, so Barnes & Noble, was put up for sale. That same year, Leonard Riggio, the genius behind today's Barnes & Noble Company, managed to convince bankers to lend him $1.2 million to purchase Barnes & Noble, an ailing bookstore on lower Fifth Avenue (at 18th Street). He brought it back to life with a humorous TV campaign and by overhauling management and inventory.[3]

Riggio immediately adopted the Barnes & Noble name for his company, a wise move that he never regretted. In fact, it has been said that he told a friend that the Barnes & Noble name alone was worth the $1.2 million he had paid for the company.

Riggio ran the store as a family business, much as Clifford Noble had done years before.

Today the New York City based Barnes & Noble, a company founded, owned, and operated by booksellers, is the world's largest bookseller, and it is growing faster than most of the major retailers in America. As of May 2005, the company operated 671 Barnes & Noble stores and 150 B. Dalton stores in fifty states and the District of Columbia.[4]

Leonard Riggio, the smart, aggressive poor boy from Brooklyn, revolutionized, and continues to revolutionize bookselling in today's unpredictable and ever-changing world. He is an extraordinary visionary and entrepreneur whose ambition and innovative concepts have made Barnes & Noble a household word; a true American icon. Through his entrepreneurship, he has helped to keep the Noble legacy alive.

Were Clifford Noble alive today, he'd certainly be astounded at what the highly controversial but very impressive Lenny Riggio, the chief executive officer of Barnes & Noble, Inc., has been able to accomplish despite his modest beginnings and the seemingly insurmountable challenges that he faced along the way.

And I bet he would be reminded of what Will Rogers had to say: "Nothing impresses 'common folk' like somebody that ain't common."

Funny thing, though…I guess that describes both Leonard and Clifford pretty well!

Sources and Notes

INTRODUCTION
1. "An Obituary Note," *The Publishers Weekly,* June 13, 1936.
2. "Harvard Class Reports, 1886, 11th Report". (Cambridge, Mass: Harvard University, 1936), pp. 312-313.

Chapter 1: THE BUDDING ENTREPRENEUR
In conducting my research, I enjoyed countless conversations with my father, J. Kendrick Noble, about his father, and about the qualities that made Pa Pa what he was. Especially helpful in writing this chapter was the unpublished memoir, "A Trip Down Union Street from 1867 to 1894," which Howard Noble wrote about growing up in Westfield, Massachusetts with his older brother, Clifford. The memoir, part of this author's collection, documents many fascinating tales about Howard's formative years with Clifford. These tales were often amplified, expanded, and enriched by details that Clifford shared with my father that confirmed Clifford's participation with his brother, Howard, in the many anecdotal adventure presented in that paper.

I also received invaluable insights and first-hand information about Clifford from his youngest daughter, Vivien Noble Wakeman, and his daughter-in-law, my mother, Orrel Baldwin Noble. My mother's father, Jay B. Baldwin, was president of the Laurel Book Company of Chicago and was a close friend of both the Noble and Barnes families.

1. Howard G. Noble, "A Trip Down United Street from 1887 to 1894" (Westfield, Mass.), 30.
2. Ibid., 5.
3. Ibid., 5.
4. Ibid., 6.
5. Ibid., 21.

Chapter 2: ROOTS
This chapter relies on information preserved in Lucius Boltwood's *Genealogy of the Family of Thomas Noble* (1878), as well as material from *The Westfield Athe-*

naeum; *The Courage of Sarah Noble* (1954), by Alice Dalgliesh; *The History of Western Massachusetts* (1855), Volumes I and II, by Josiah Gilbert Holland; and conversations with family members. Men and women of character have always found their way into the historical record and Clifford's ancestor Thomas Noble is a case in point.

1. Luis Boltwood, *History and Genealogy of the Family of Thomas Noble* (Hartford, Conn.: Lockwood & Brainard Company, 1878), 19.

2. Ibid.,19.

3. Ibid., 19.

4. Ibid., 26.

5. Ibid., 20.

6. Ibid., 20.

7. Ibid., 20.

8. Josiah Gilbert Holland, *History of Western Massachusetts, 2 Vols.* (Springfield, Mass.: Samuel Bowles & Co., 1855), 1: 66.

9. The Westfield Athenaeum, *Images of America, Vol II* (Westfield, Mass.: Chalford Publishing Corp., 1997), Introduction.

10. Lockwood, John H.D.D., Rev., *Westfield and its Historic Influences 1669–1919, 2 vols.* (Salem, Mass.: Higginson Book Co., 1922), 2:482.

11. Boltwood, op.cit., 21.

12. Ibid., 21.

13. Ibid., 21.

14. Ibid., 21.

Chapter 3: WESTFIELD AS HOME

Several Noble & Noble titles—Whalen and Baldwin's *Complete United States History Text-Workbook* (1953), Baldwin's *The Story of Our America* (1960), and Parkhill's *Complete History of Our United States* (1961), the New York Amsterdam News (October 7, 2005–March 6, 2006), as well as Tyner's *President Abraham Lincoln* (1961)—were all useful sources of historical information for this chapter. So too were the works by Lockwood, Holland and, Boltwood listed in the Bibliography.

1. Boltwood, op.cit., 496.

2. Ibid., 496.

3. Christopher L. Tyner, "President Abraham Lincoln," *Investor's Business Daily*, February 20, 2001.

4. Rev. John H. Lockwood, 2 vols., op.cit., 1: 423.
5. Ibid., 424.
6. Ibid., 428.
7. Ibid., 429.
8. Ibid., pp. 445-446

Chapter 4: BIRTH AND EARLY YEARS
We are fortunate to know as much as we do about Clifford Noble's early years. Personal recollections of family members, such as Howard Noble's memoir "A Trip Down Union Street," as retold by Clifford, and more formalized genealogies such as Lucius Boltwood's work, provide more background for the portrait of Clifford that emerged in this chapter. Additional historical detail is found in *The Westfield Athenaeum*'s contribution to the *Images of America* series.

1. Howard G. Noble, op.cit., 12.
2. The Westfield Athenaeum, op.cit., 2.
3. Ibid., 1.
4. Howard G. Noble, op.cit., 13.
5. Ibid., 18.
6. Ibid., 18.
7. Ibid., 18.
8. Ibid., 15.

Chapter 5: DREAMS OF COLLEGE
Both of Clifford's parents, and his teachers in the Westfield public schools, fostered his love of books and learning at an early age. The more Clifford learned, the more he wanted to learn, and his steadfast determination to attend Harvard clearly illustrates his lifelong ability to focus on the goal worth winning. This largely anecdotal chapter took the slim outline of events at the time and fills in the gaps with Clifford's likely thoughts and actions as he pursued his dream. Some of these impressions however, are truly his own, having been written into the biographical narrative that Clifford prepared for his fiftieth Harvard class reunion.

1. John Ferling, *A Life—John Adams* (New York: Henry Holt & Company, 1992), 15.
2. Abbot Lawrence Lowell et al., *The History and Traditions of Harvard College* (Cambridge, Mass.: The Harvard Crimson, 1929), 66.

Chapter 6: HARVARD COLLEGE
Information about the Harvard experience that was typical of many students in Clifford's day has been amply recorded, and especially well, by sources consulted for this chapter. In addition to those credited in the text, Harvard student John Ulrich's research in the "1886 Harvard Class Reports," John Bethell's *Harvard Observed*, and Abbot Lawrence Lowell's *The History and Traditions of Harvard College* were exceptionally informative.

1. Abbot Lawrence Lowell, *The History and Traditions of Harvard College* (Cambridge, Mass.: The Harvard Crimson, 1929), 23.
2. Ibid., 29.
3. Ibid., 33.
4. John T. Bethell, *Harvard Observed* (Cambridge, Mass.: Harvard University Press, 1998), 22.
5 John Ferling, op.cit., 15.
6. Lowell et al., 28.
7. Ibid., 30.
8. John Uhlrich, "Letters and Reports," (Cambridge, Mass.: Harvard Class Report, 1886).
10. Ibid.
11. Ibid.
12. Nancy Sirkis, *Boston* (New York: The Viking Press, 1966), 84.
13. Uhlrich, op.cit.
14. Sirkis, op.cit., 84.

Chapter 7: NEW YORK CITY
The E. B. White epigraph at the beginning of this chapter was found in Marqusee and Harris's *New York*, and it seems especially appropriate there. Research for this chapter was aided greatly by reference to Crichton's *America 1900*; Witheridge's *New York, Then and Now*; Anderson's *Bookselling in America*; The *Personal Recollections* of John Barnes Pratt, Tebbel's *A History of Book Publishing in the United States*, Bowker's *Lectures on Book Publishing*; The *Publishers Weekly* 1936, "An Obituary Note", James D. McCabe Jr.'s *New York By Gaslight* and Clifford Noble's own biographical narrative.

1. Stephen Birmingham, *Life at the Dakota* (New York: Random House, 1979), 5.
2. Annette Witheridge, *New York, Then and Now* (San Diego, Calif.: Thunder Bay Press, 2001), 6.
3. Judy Crichton, *America in 1900* (New York: Henry Holt & Co., 1998), 70.
4. Witheridge, op.cit., 6.
5. Birmingham, op.cit., 8.
6. Geoffrey Faber, A *Publisher Speaking* (New York: Houghton Mifflin Co., 1935), 22.
7. John Barnes Pratt, *Personal Recollections—Sixty Years of Book Publishing* (New York: A.S. Barnes and Co., 1942), 17.
8. James D. McCabe, Jr., *New York By Gaslight* (New York: Greenwich House, 1984), 308.

Chapter 8: A CHANCE ENCOUNTER IN CENTRAL PARK

The author's conversations with Clifford's youngest daughter, Vivien Noble Wakeman, provided much of the details about Lizzie's initial chance encounter with Clifford Noble in Central Park.

1. Birmingham, op.cit., 142.

Chapter 9: FROM HOLIDAYS TO PARTNERSHIPS

Hunter's *The Family of William Adams,* Trumbull's *History of Bergen and Passaic Counties,* and Henry Adams's obituary in *American Silk Journal* were invaluable in providing details of Lizzie's family background. Descriptions of "the wedding of the century" were found in the *Westfield Times and News Letter* for January 13, 1892.

1. Crichton, op.cit., 278.
2. William Adams Hunter IV, "The Family of William Adams," 76.
3. Ibid., 86.
4. *A History of Industrial Patterson New Jersey* (Patterson, N.J.: Carleton M. Herrick, Book and Job Printer, 1882), pp 208-212.
5. Sheryl A. Kujawa-Holbrooks, *By Grace Came the Incarnation* (New York: Church of the Incarnation, 2004), 70.
6. Ibid., 84.
7. *Times and Newsletter*—January 13, 1892 (Westfield, Mass.)

Chapter 10: YONKERS, NEW YORK
Much of the historical detail about activities in Yonkers was derived from sources such as Philip Pistone's *Landmarks Lost and Found: An Introduction to the Architecture and History of Yonkers* and Henry Brown's *Old Yonkers: 1646–1922*. Credit is also due Kendrick Noble's 1970 article "Where Have All the Great Ones Gone?" and Mary Panzer's *In My Studio–Rudolph Eickemeyer, Jr. and the Art of the Camera, 1855–1930*.

1. Philip R. Pistone, *Landmarks Lost & Found: An Introduction to the Architecture and History of Yonkers* (Yonkers, N.Y.: Planning and Development Commission), An Overview—1.
2. Ibid.
3. Henry Collins Brown, *Old Yonkers: 1646–1922* (New York: The Yonkers Trust Company, 1922), 15-27.
4. Pistone, op.cit., 1.
5. Ibid., 13.
6. Ibid., 20.
7. Mary Panzer, *In My Studio—Rudolph Eickemeyer, Jr. and the Art of the Camera. 1855–1930* (Yonkers, N.Y.: The Hudson River Museum, 1986).

Chapter 11: LIFE WITH FATHER
The anecdotal material included in this chapter was adapted from personal conversations with Vivien Noble Wakeman, J. Kendrick Noble, Orrel Baldwin Noble, and other family members as well as from the author's personal observations.

Chapter 12: THANKSGIVING AND CHRISTMAS
This chapter's descriptions of the warmth, tradition, fun, and excitement of Thanksgiving and Christmas are drawn largely from the memories of Clifford's children Vivien Noble Wakeman and J. Kendrick Noble. The author's mother, Orrel Baldwin Noble, and other family members also contributed to this remembrance of holidays past.

Chapter 13: VACATIONS
Natalie Moore Montgomery's *A Century of Beach Houses* was helpful in preparing this chapter, as was the *Fire Island News* and my many conversations with Clifford's family members.

1. *Fire Island News* (Ocean Beach, N.Y., 1963), 31.
2. Ibid.
3. Ibid.
4. Natalie Moore Montgomery, *A Century of Beach Houses* (New York: The Point O'Woods Historical Society, 1995).
5. Ibid.
6. John Bartlett, *Bartlett's Familiar Quotations* (Boston, Mass.: Little Brown & Company, 1980), 844.

Chapter 14: THE FOUNDING OF BARNES & NOBLE
Important historical information for this chapter was found in Clifford's biographical narrative and Kendrick Noble's "The Good Old Days." Other sources included *The Publishers Weekly's*, "An Obituary Note on Clifford Noble," Wolfe's *The House of Appleton*, Tebbel's *Between Covers* and *A History of Book Publishing in the United States*. Further information was obtained from *Follett's Library Services*, "Follett: Our History," www.westlaw.com (regarding Clifford's legal action in the Hinds, Noble & Eldredge dispute), and e-mail correspondence from Bob Follett and Steve Waichler.

1. Gerald Wolfe, *The House of Appleton* (Metuchen, N.J.: The Scarecrow Press, Inc., 1981), 324.
2. John Tebbel, *A History of Book Publishing in the United States, 3 vols.* (New York: R.R. Bowker, 1975), 2:60.
3. John Tebbel, *Between Covers* (New York: Oxford University Press, 1987), 83.
4. Tebbel, op.cit., pp. 2:95-96.
5. Wolfe, op.cit., 328.
6. John Tebbel, *A History of Book Publishing in the United States*, op.cit., 2:93.
7. "A Brief History of Follett Corporation" (Chicago, Ill., 1986, Follett Corporation, 1986).

Chapter 15: NOBLE & NOBLE
In addition to sources credited in the text, Kendrick Noble's "The Good Old Days" and Clifford's biographical narrative were especially useful in writing this chapter. For the thirty years following Clifford's death, Noble & Noble continued to be a formidable player in the publishing industry. Sources used to write this chapter include the June 13, 1936 edition of *The Publishers Weekly*, Wolfe's *The House of Appleton*, Tebbel's *Between Covers*, conversations with family mem-

bers, and a 1967 article on Kendrick Noble's retirement in the Bronxville, New York, *Review Press-Reporter.*

1. Wolfe, op.cit., 360.
2. John Tebbel, *Between Covers* (New York: Oxford University Press, 1987), 275.
3. Wolfe, op.cit., 361.

Chapter 16: THE PASSING OF A LEGEND
Information for this chapter was secured from the "Kensico" brochure provided by Kensico Cemetery, *The Publishers Weekly's*, June 13, 1936, "An Obituary Note" on Clifford Noble, Robert Cusick Noble's "Noble Genealogy," and the June and October 1988 issues of *Spy* magazine.

1. Jack Barth, "The Spy Trip Tip," *Spy* (New York: Spy Publishing Partners, June, 1988).
2. Noble, Anne R., Esq. "Dear Editors," *Spy* (New York: Spy Publishing Partners, October, 1988), 25.
3. Ibid., 25.

Chapter 17: THE LEGACY
Clifford's legacy was dictated by the simple principles he lived by; his value system and his priorities, all of which contributed to his stunning success as a family man and business leader in the book industry.

REORGANIZATION AND RENEWAL
Following the sale of Barnes & Noble, Clifford continued to build and expand Noble & Noble until it was recognized as one of the foremost small publishing companies in the nation. Information for this chapter was found in several articles and publications including "Noble & Noble Elects Officers," Tebbel's *Between Covers* and *A History of Book Publishing in the United States*, Wolfe's *The House of Appleton*, and articles from *The New York Times* ("Textbook House Bought By Dell") and the *Bronxville Review Press Reporter*, ("J. Kendrick Noble Feted On Retirement"). Also of special importance was Follett's Library Services and e-mail correspondences from Bob Follett and Steve Waichler.

1. Harry Gilroy, "Textbook House Bought By Dell", *New York Times* (New York: R.R. Bowker Company, 1975), pp. 220-221.

2. John Tebbel, *A History of Book Publishing in the United States, 3 vols.* (New York: R.R. Bowker Company, 1978), 3:220.

3. Cover Story: "The Baron of Books," New York: *Business Week*—McGraw Hill Companies, June 29, 1998.

4. "Barnes & Noble First Quarter Financial Results, Press Release"—May 17, 2005.

A FINAL POSTSCRIPT: Clifford Noble's sister and younger brother, both life-time residents of Westfield, followed him in death. Julia, married to Edward Rochwood, died in 1953. Howard, married to Hattie Bates, retired from the Howard G. Noble Insurance Agency in 1940. He died in 1956.

Bibliography

"About the Cooper Union." www.augustachronicle.com, Oct. 24, 2002.

Adams, Henry. *The Education of Henry Adams*. New York: The Modern Library, 1999.

Alpert, Lukas et al., "Story of the Century: How Papers Covered Calendar's Change—1899 and Now." *North County Times*. San Diego, California: Dec. 26, 1999.

American Silk Journal. Vol. 9, Number 6, "Henry Adams Obituary." New York: The Rose and Trumbull Co. Publishers, June 1890.

Anderson, Charles B. *Bookselling in America and the World*. New York: Quadrangle. The New York Times Book Company, 1975.

"Annual Report 2002—New York." New York: Barnes & Noble Inc., 2001.

Antoniou, Jim. *Cities, Then and Now*. Edison, New Jersey: Chartwell Books, 1994.

Baldwin, Orrel T. *The Story of Our America*. New York City: Noble & Noble Publishers Inc., 1960.

Baldwin, Orrel T. and B. E. Strumpf. *New York. Past and Present*. New York: Noble & Noble Publishing Company, 1964.

"Barnes & Noble Reports Comparable Store Sales for September." New York: Barnes and Noble Inc., Oct. 10, 2002.

"Barnes & Noble Reports First Quarter Financial Results," May 17, 2005. www.barnesandnobleinc.com/press-releases/2005.

Barnes, W. R. "Genesis of Jobbing." *The College Store Journal.* Winter Issue, 1960.

Barth, Jack. "The Spy Trip Tip." *Spy.* New York: New York Spy Publishing Partners, June 1988.

Bartlett, John. *Bartlett's Familiar Quotations.* Boston: Little Brown and Company, 1980.

Berss, Marcia. "A Family Affair." *Forbes.* March 27, 1995.

Bethell, John T. *Harvard Observed.* Cambridge, Massachusetts: Harvard University Press, 1998.

Birmingham, Stephen. *Life at the Dakota.* New York: Random House, 1979.

Boltwood, Lucius. *Genealogy of the Family of Thomas Noble.* Hartford, Connecticut: Press of the Case, Lockwood & Brainard Company, 1878.

Bookman, Mark. "College Store Journal." *College Store Newsletter.* Professional Management Associates, April 1992.

Bowker Lectures on Book Publishing. New York: R. R. Bowker Company, 1957.

A Brief History of Follett Corporation. Chicago, Illinois: Follett Corporation, June 1986.

Brown, Henry Collins. *Fifth Avenue Old and New, 1824–1924.* New York: The Fifth Avenue Association, 1924.

Brown, Henry Collins. *Old Yonkers: 1646–1922.* New York: The Yonkers Trust Company. New York: The Valentines Manual Press, 1922.

Buss, Dale. "Book Learning." *Context Magazine.* September–October, 1999. www.contextmag.com/archives/1999/Feature1booklearning.asp.

Catton, Bruce. *Reflections on the Civil War.* New York: Berkley Books, 1981.

Champlin, Ken. "Underground Railroad Historic Trail Proposed." *South Coast Today,* Oct. 12, 2002.

Cohen, Sharon. "Papers Captured Century Spirit." Augusta, Georgia: *The Augusta Chronicle,* Dec. 30, 1999.

Cover Story: "The Baron of Books." New York: *Business Week*—McGraw Hill Companies, June 29, 1998.

Crichton, Judy. *America 1900.* New York: Henry Holt & Company, 1998.

Dalgliesh, Alice. *The Courage of Sarah Noble.* New York: Charles Scribner & Sons, 1954.

Dessauer, John P. *Book Publishing.* New York: Continuum, 1999.

Devine, James E. *Our New York.* New York: Noble & Noble Publishers Inc., 1961.

"Discover a Heroic Heritage Along the Underground Railroad." TownNews.com

Edmonds, Cyrus R. *Cicero's Essays on Old Age and Friendship.* New York: Hinds & Noble.

Egan, Robert. *The Bookstore of Books.* New York: Avon Books, 1979.

Entrepreneur.com. "Barnes & Noble. Build A Better Mousetrap." www.entrepreneur.com/Magazines/MA. Oct. 18, 2002.
———. "How To Build A Million-Dollar Business—Barnes & Noble." www.entrepreneur-online.com, Oct. 18, 2002.

Epstein, Jason. *Book Business.* New York: W. W. Norton & Company, 2001.

Faber, Geoffrey. *A Publisher Speaking.* Boston and New York: Houghton Mifflin Company, 1935.

Ferling, John. *John Adams—A Life.* New York: Henry Holt & Company, 1992.

The Fifth Avenue Association Inc. *Fifth Avenue Old and New*. New York: Wynkoop, Hallenbeck Crawford Company, 1924.

"Fire Island Guide." Ocean Beach, New York: Trigar Publishing Company Inc., 1966.

Fire Island News. Ocean Beach, New York, 1963.

Flandreau, Charles Macomb. *The Diary of a Freshman*. New York: D. Appleton-Century Co., 1938.

Flynn, Tom. "A Century Later, Much Remains the Same." *The Quarterly Journal of the Yonkers Historical Society*. Vol. 7, No. 3. Fall, 1998.
————. *Yonkers Life in 1900*. Yonkers, New York: Yonkers Historical Society, 2000.

Follett, Bob. *E-Mail-Personal Communication*. November 2002.

"Follett History." *Follett Library Resources*.

"Follett: Our History." Follett High Education Group, Oct. 17, 2002.

Gilbert, Martin. *A History of the Twentieth Century*. New York: Avon Books, 1997.

Gilroy, Harry. "Textbook House Bought By Dell." *The New York Times*. New York, 1965.

Gray, Christopher. *Fifth Avenue, 1911 from Start to Finish*. New York: Dover Publications Inc., 1994.

Haberlin, Thomas. *The Westfield Historic Building Book*. Westfield Community Development Commission, 1981.

Hackett, Alice Payne. *70 Years of Best Sellers—1895–1965*. New York: R. R. Bowker Company, 1967.

Hall, Donald. *The Education of Henry Adams*. New York: Houghton Mifflin Company, 2002.

"Harvard Class Reports, 1886, 11th Report." Cambridge, Massachusetts: Harvard University, 1936. Harvard Depository (HUD 286.505, Box 298), 50th Class Anniversary folder.

Hemingway, Ernest. *A Moveable Feast*. 1964 epigraph. New York: Scribner Book Company, 1996.

"Historic and Scenic Tour. The Kensico Cemetery—1889." Valhalla, New York: Kensico Cemetery.

Holland, Josiah Gilbert. *History of Western Massachusetts*. Springfield, Massachusetts: Samuel Bowles & Company, 1855.

Homberger, Eric. *The Historical Atlas of New York City*. New York: Henry Holt & Company, 2005.

"How To Build A Million Dollar Business—Barnes & Noble." *Entrepreneur.com,* November 2002.

Hunter, William Adams, IV. *The Family of William Adams*. 2003 Edition. "The Independent Books To Read: The Industries, Issues, and Superstores."

Johnson, Madeline C. *Fire Island*. Mountainside, New Jersey: Shoreland Press, 1983.

Kazak, Don. "For the eyes and mind." *Palo Alto Weekly*, Dec. 2, 1998.

"Kensico." Valhalla, New York: Kensico Cemetery.

Kirkpatrick, David D. "A Shifting of Leadership at Bookseller." *New York Times*, Feb. 14, 2002.
———. "Barnes & Noble's Jekyll and Hyde." *New York Magazine*, July 19, 1999.

Klemesrud, Judy. "A Summer Colony That Is an Island Unto Itself and Enjoys It. *New York Times*, July 28, 1968, p. 58.

Klingaman, William K. *Abraham Lincoln*. New York: Viking, 2001.

Kneerim, Arthur. *Old New York: Our Neighborhood*. New York: The New York Savings Bank, 1932.

Knopf, Alfred A. *Publishing Then and Now—1912–1964*. New York: The New York Public Library, 1964.

Korda, Michael. *Making the List*. New York: Barnes & Noble, 2001.

Kujawa-Holbrook, Sheryl A. *By Grace Came the Incarnation: A Social History of the Incarnation*. Murray Hill, 1852–2002. New York: Church of the Incarnation, 2004.

Lockridge, Kenneth A. *A New England Town: The First Hundred Years*. New York: W. W. Norton & Company Inc., 1970.

Lockwood, D. D. Reverend John H. *Westfield and His Historic Influences—1669–1919*. Salem, Massachusetts: Higginson Book Company, 1922.

Lowell, Abbot Lawrence et al. "The History and Traditions of Harvard College." *The Harvard Crimson*. Cambridge, Massachusetts, 1929.

Madison, Charles A. *Book Publishing in America*. New York: McGraw Hill Book Company, 1966.

Marqusee, Mike and Bill Harris. *New York*. New York: Barnes & Noble, 1985.

Massey, Mary Elizabeth. *Women in the Civil War*. Nebraska: University of Nebraska, 1966.

McDermott, Edward J. *The Westfield Historic Building Book*. Westfield, Massachusetts: Westfield Community Development Commission, 1981.

McCabe, James D. *New York By Gaslight*. New York: Greenwich House, 1964.

Meinig, D. W. *The Shaping of America.* New Haven, Connecticut: Yale University Press, 1986.

Melcher, Frederic G. *Friendly Reminiscences.* New York: The Book Publishers' Bureau, 1945.

Montgomery, Natalie Moore. *A Century of Beach Houses.* New York: The Point O'Woods Historical Society, 1995.

Morgan, Charles. *The House of Macmillan.* London: Macmillan & Co. Ltd., 1943.

Morrison, Samuel Eliot. *Three Centuries of Harvard—1636–1936.* New York: Houghton Mifflin.

Mumby, Frank. *Publishing and Bookselling.* London: Jonathon Cape, 1854.
Munk, Nina. "Title Fight." *Fortune.* June 21, 1999.

"Noble-Adams Wedding." *Times and News Letter.* Westfield, Massachusetts, Jan. 13, 1892.

"Noble and Noble Elects Officers." *Publishers Weekly,* 1936.

Noble, Anne R., Esq. "Dear Editors." *Spy.* New York: Spy Publishing Partners, Oct. 1988.

Noble, G. Clifford. Biographical Narrative. Dec. 19, 1935.

Noble, Howard G. "A Trip Down Union Street from 1887 to 1894." Westfield, Massachusetts: Westfield Athenaeum, 1949. (Unpublished private collection: Betty Noble Turner.)

Noble, J. Kendrick. "News Flash." *Bookbinding and Book Production,* March 1950.

Noble, J. Kendrick. *Educational Books We Publish.* New York: Noble & Noble Publishers Inc., 1922.

———. "Feted on Retirement." *Review Press-Reporter*, April 13, 1967.
———. "Former Publisher." *The New York Times*, Nov. 17, 1978.
———.
———. *The Old (Good) Days*. Bronxville, New York, 1975. Unpublished. (Betty Noble Turner collection.)
———.Personal conversations, 1960–1985.
———"Where Have All The Great Ones Gone?" Yonkers, New York: *Yonkers Historical Bulletin*. Vol. XV11, #1, January 1970.

Noble, James Kendrick Jr. Personal conversations, 2000.

Noble, Orrel Baldwin. Personal conversations. Texas: 1970–1997.

Noble, Robert Cusick. "Noble Genealogy." Philadelphia, Pennsylvania: July 17, 1991. (Unpublished private collection of Betty Noble Turner.)

Noble, Stanley R. *Speeches*. (Betty Noble Turner Collection.)

"Noble and Noble Elects Officers." *Publishers Weekly*, 1936.

Norrington, A. L. P. *Blackwell's, 1879–1979*. Oxford: Blackwell, 1983.

"An Obituary Note—G. Clifford Noble." *The Publishers Weekly*, June 13, 1936.
"Obituary—G. Kingsley Noble." *Herald Tribune*, Dec. 10, 1940.
"An Obituary—Henry Adams." *The American Silk Journal*, June 1890.
"Obituary—Henry Adams." *Dry Good Economist*, June 7, 1890.
Obituary—"Howard Noble Dies at Age 89 in Westfield." *Westfield Newspaper*, Nov. 9, 1956.
"Obituary—James Noble." *Westfield News Letter*, March 1, 1900.
"Obituary—James Noble." *The Women's Journal*, March 24, 1900.
Obituary—James Kendrick Noble. *The Austin Citizen*, Nov. 21, 1978.
Obituary—James Kendrick Noble. *New York Times*, Nov. 17, 1978.

Ojito, Mirta. "Deep Roots Guarantee a Bookseller's Independence." *New York Times*, Nov. 19, 2002.

Orioli, G. *Adventures of a Bookseller*. New York: Robert M. McBride & Company, 1938.

Panzer, Mary. *In My Studio: Rudolf Eickemeyer Jr. and the Art of the Camera. 1855–1930.* Yonkers, New York: The Hudson River Museum, 1986.

Parkhill, Wilson. *Complete History of Our United States.* New York: Noble & Noble Publishers Inc., 1961.

Pioneer Valley Planning Commission. "Community—Westfield. West Springfield Massachusetts." Pioneer Valley Planning Commission, April 1998.

Pistone, Philip R. *Landmarks Lost & Found: An Introduction to the Architecture and History of Yonkers.* Yonkers, New York: Planning and Development Commission.

"Point O'Woods, Fire Island." BarrierBeaches.com, Nov. 24, 2002.

Pratt, John Barnes. *Personal Recollections—Sixty Years of Book Publishing.* New York: A. S. Barnes and Company, 1942.

Pringle, Henry F. *Theodore Roosevelt—A Biography.* New York: Harcourt Brace & Company, 1956.

Pruitt, Bettye H. *The Making of Harcourt General.* Boston: Harvard Business School Press, 1994.

Raff, Daniel M. G. "Revolution in the Book Trade (B): Barnes & Noble." University of Pennsylvania: The Wharton School—Center for Leadership and Case Management, Jan. 15, 2000.

Raymond, Cornelia M. *Memories of a Child of Vassar.* New York: Vassar College, 1940.

Reynolds, Russell. "College Store Newsletter." Oberlin Ohio: Professional Management Associates, 1992.

Riggio, Leonard. "Superstores Are Not Predators." *Publishers Weekly,* Nov. 9, 1992.

"The Riggio Manifesto." *Publishers Weekly,* April 3, 2000.

Roosevelt, David B. *Grandmere.* New York, 2002.

Sanders, Charles W. *Sanders Union Reader.* New York: Ivison, Blakeman & Company, 1801.

Seuss, Dr. *Oh, The Places You'll Go.* New York: Random House, 1990.

Sheehan, Donald H. *This is America My Country.* Veterans Historical Book Services Inc., 1952.

Siebert, Wilber H. "The Underground Railroad in Massachusetts." American Antiquation Society.

Shurter, Edwin Dubois. *Patriotic Selections.* New York: Lloyd Adams Noble, 1918.

Siebert, Wilber H. *The Underground Railroad in Massachusetts.* American Antiquation Society.

Simpson, Alan. *Helen Lockwood's College Years, 1908–1912.* Poughkeepsie, New York: Vassar College, 1977.

Sims, Bobbi. *Don't Let 'em Crumble Your Cookies.* Corpus Christi, Texas: Elan Publishing, 1998.

Sirkis, Nancy. *Boston.* New York: The Viking Press, 1963.

Smith, Richard Norton. New York: *The Harvard Century.* New York: Houghton Mifflin.

Stack, Herbert J. and Esther Z. Schwartz. *Safety Every Day.* New York: Noble & Noble Publishers Inc., 1939.

Tebbel, John A. *Between Covers.* New York: Oxford University Press, 1987.
———. *A History of Book Publishing in the United States,* 4 Vols. New York: R. R. Bowker Company, 1978.

The New York Amsterdam News, October 7, 2005–March 5, 2006.

Tifft, Susan E. and Alex S. Jones. *The Trust.* New York: Little Brown & Company, 1999.

Times and Newsletter. Westfield, Massachusetts, 1864.

Trachtenberg, Jeffrey A. "Barnes & Noble's Stephen Riggio To Become CEO." *The Wall Street Journal*, Feb. 14, 2002.

Trumbull, L. R. *History of Bergen and Passaic Counties, New Jersey.* Carleton M. Herrick Book and Job Printer, 1882.
———. *A History of Industrial Patterson.* Patterson, New Jersey: Carleton M. Herrick, Book and Job Printer, 1882.

Tyner, Christopher L. "President Abraham Lincoln." New York: *Investor's Business Daily*, Feb. 20, 2001.

Ulrich, John. Letters and Reports. *Harvard Class Reports, 1886.* Cambridge, Massachusetts, 1999.

Waichler, Nancy Follett. Personal e-mail. Oct. 2, 2002.

Waichler, Steve. Personal e-mail. Oct. 2, 2002.

Wakeman, Vivien Noble. Personal conversations. 1998–2001.
———. "Letter to Betty Turner." Oct. 3, 1999.

Waring, Belle. "The Struggle of the Independent Bookseller." AWP: The Associated Writing Programs. www.awpwriter.org. Oct. 18, 2002.

Web site. www.westlaw.com

Westfield Athenaeum. "Images of America: Westfield." Dover, New Hampshire: Chalford Publishing Corporation, 1997.

Westfield Athenaeum. "Images of America", Vol. 2. Dover, New Hampshire: Chalford Publishing Corporation, 1997.

Westfield Chamber of Commerce. "The Romantic Horse and Buggy Period." Westfield, Massachusetts.

Westfield Chamber News. Westfield, Massachusetts. Summer 1998. *Westfield News Letter,* 1861.

Weybright, Victor. *The Making of a Publisher.* New York: Reynal & Company, 1966.

Whalen, Frank D. and Orrel T. Baldwin, *Complete United States History Text-Workbook.* New York: Noble & Noble Publishers, 1953.

Witheridge, Annette. *New York, Then and Now.* San Diego, California: Thunder Bay Press, 2001.

Wolfe, Gerald. *The House of Appleton.* Metuchen, New Jersey: The Scarecrow Press Inc., 1981.

Yonkers Board of Trade. "Yonkers Illustrated." Salem, Massachusetts: Higginson Book Company reprint.

The Yonkers Historical Society Newsletter. Yonkers, New York: The Yonkers Historical Society.

About the Author

Betty Noble Turner is a long-term veteran of the book publishing and bookselling industry. Her maternal and paternal grandfathers were presidents of their respective book companies in Chicago (The Laurel Book Company) and in New York City (Barnes & Noble Inc.), and her father was president of Noble & Noble Inc., one of the earlier, better known New York-based textbook publishing companies.

Following her graduation from Vassar College, Betty Noble Turner served as a book editor and Texas sales manager at Noble & Noble. She secured state and local textbook adoptions in Texas while completing her graduate degree from Texas A & I. She later served two terms as the first female mayor of Corpus Christi, Texas; was publicly honored by her hometown of Yonkers, New York, and was elected to the national AARP board. She has received countless honors and awards for her many years of public, professional, volunteer, and political service.

Betty currently serves as broker and owner of the Betty Turner Real Estate Company, which has offices in Port Aransas and Corpus Christi, Texas. She is an elder in the Presbyterian Church, a board member for several not-for-profit agencies, and a freelance writer. *The Noble Legacy* is her first book.

Betty, a native of New York, currently resides in South Texas with her husband, award-winning architect Jack Rice Turner. Jack and Betty's two sons, Jay and Randall and their families, live in Dallas.

978-0-595-67508-1
0-595-67508-5

Printed in the United States
46464LVS00007B/25-42